Praise for Damian

'I remember how it felt as a young child to be told that I was losing my hearing. I was scared, worried and concerned. I soon realised there was no point in mourning the loss of my hearing but instead I began to find excitement in discovering new ways to change. Damian Hughes tells you how to make the same journey.'

Dame Evelyn Glennie, classical musician

'The world depends on people who are prepared to challenge conventions and accepted wisdom. Damian Hughes can give you the necessary courage to do so.'

Sir Roger Bannister

'I would encourage you to listen to Damian Hughes, implement his ideas and then enjoy being amazed at the power you possess to become a true change catalyst.'

Tim Smit CBE, founder of The Eden Project

'I defy anyone not to be inspired and moved by Damian's belief in people and their potential.'

Kim Morgan, Managing Director, Barefoot Coaching

'Damian Hughes is a catalyst to help you take the steps required to creating real, lasting and sustainable change in your life or in the world about you.'

Tom Bloxham MBE, entrepreneur

'Using thought-provoking and inspiring stories Damian has challenged and inspired us and more importantly given us a common language which we all can use.'

Emma Mirrington, Head of Talent, Mars Chocolate UK

'I've learned that you only get out of life what you are prepared to put in. If you are prepared to listen to Damian with an eager and open mind, you will be successful.'

Steve Williams, caddy to Tiger Woods

'I would encourage you to use Damian to challenge and make you think about situations in your life where you can take a lead, whatever your current status or position. You will surprise yourself with your true abilities.'

Bill Sweetenham, National Performance Director, Great Britain swimming team

'Damian Hughes captures many important lessons about how to deal with change. I have no hesitation in recommending him as a fantastic guide to accompany you on your own journey.'

Tony Smith, Head Coach, Warrington Wolves, England and Great Britain national rugby league team

How to Change Absolutely Anything

How to Change Absolutely Anything

DAMIAN HUGHES

Harlow, England • London • New York • Boston • San Francisco • Toronto • Sydney • Auckland • Singapore • Hong Kong
Tokyo • Seoul • Taipei • New Delhi • Cape Town • São Paulo • Mexico City • Madrid • Amsterdam • Munich • Paris • Milan

PEARSON EDUCATION LIMITED
Edinburgh Gate
Harlow CM20 2JE
Tel: +44 (0)1279 623623
Fax: +44 (0)1279 431059
Website: www.pearson.com/uk

First published in Great Britain in 2012

Pearson Education is not responsible for the content of third-party internet sites.

ISBN: 978-0-273-77091-6

British Library Cataloguing-in-Publication Data
A catalogue record for this book is available from the British Library

Library of Congress Cataloging-in-Publication Data
Hughes, Damian.
  How to change absolutely anything / Damian Hughes.
    p. cm.
  ISBN 978-0-273-77091-6 (pbk.)
  1. Self-help techniques. 2. Self-confidence. 3. Life skills. I. Title.

  BF632.H84 2012
  158--dc23
                            2012013154

10 9 8 7 6 5 4 3 2 1
16 15 14 13 12

Cartoons by Bill Piggins
Typeset in 10/13pt ITC Giovanni Book by 30
Printed in Great Britain by Henry Ling Ltd., at the Dorset Press, Dorchester, Dorset

Contents

Introduction xi

1 Create the right first impression: approaching change in a way that makes the journey smoother 1

2 Decide how you want to be perceived: using what you say and do to win over others 11

3 Recognise the power of emotions: avoiding the emotional triggers that may jeopardise change 29

4 Address the four big needs: controlling your feelings to influence change 43

5 Understand your reaction to change: interpreting the facts of a situation to determine the outcome 65

6 Anticipate how those around you will react to change: learning to be flexible to get the support you need 75

7 Examine your beliefs: using your beliefs to promote change 93

8 **Avoid belief traps:** spotting the most common mistakes that hinder change 101

9 **Be aware of where you're sitting:** understanding what influences you to find the key to change 115

10 **Take action:** over to you... 131

Personal postscript 139

About the author

Damian Hughes is Professor of Human Resource Management and Organisational Behaviour at Manchester Metropolitan University. He is also a change management consultant, sports psychologist and founder of LiquidThinker Ltd. Working with a wide range of industries, high profile sports teams, and individuals, his innovative, engaging and effective approaches to the understanding and application of change have had clear and demonstrable impact. His work, showing how the methods of big achievers can be applied by anybody to realise ambition and reach full potential, has received significant recognition and acclaim.

Publisher's acknowledgements

We are grateful to the following for permission to reproduce copyright material:

'The Paradoxical Commandments' on pp 136–7 are reprinted by permission of the author. © Copyright Kent M. Keith 1968, renewed 2001.The Paradoxical Commandments were written by Kent M. Keith as part of his book, *The Silent Revolution: Dynamic Leadership in the Student Council*, published in 1968 by Harvard Student Agencies, Cambridge, Massachusetts. More information is available at www.paradoxicalcommandments.com

In some instances we have been unable to trace the owners of copyright material and we would appreciate any information that would enable us to do so.

Introduction

This is a book to help you change things

Maybe you want your team to do things differently at work. Perhaps you have an idea that you're struggling to get others to back. You could want to persuade your boss to agree to a proposal. Maybe you want to get your family to improve their health or communicate better. It could be that you want to change something about your child's school or the local community. Maybe it's closer to home and you want to change something very personal to you – such as get promoted or lose weight. In short, this is about any change you want to see happen.

Usually these topics are treated separately – there is 'change management' advice for businesses, 'self-help' advice for individuals and 'change the world' advice for activists. This is a shame because all change has something fundamental in common: for anything to change, someone has to start acting differently. Ultimately, all change efforts boil down to the same mission: can you start behaving in a new way and influence others to do the same?

I know what you're thinking – it's so difficult, and people resist change. But that's not always true. In our lives, we actively choose to make lots of big changes: we have babies, start new relationships, get married, move home, get a new gadget or adopt new technology, and seek out new job roles. Meanwhile, other behaviours are maddeningly resistant. Smokers keep smoking, kids grow fatter and men still forget to put the toilet seat down.

So why do we actively choose some fairly major changes, but actively resist others? And what about those special people who change everything they touch – like magic? Those who can turn something around without breaking sweat? How do they do it?

There's a story about the great artist Pablo Picasso. One day a woman spotted him in the market and pulled out a piece of paper. 'Mr Picasso,' she said excitedly, 'I'm a big fan. Please, could you do a little drawing for me?' Picasso happily complied and quickly made a sketch for her on the paper. As he handed it back, he smiled and told her to 'take care of it. That will be worth a million dollars one day.' The woman looked flustered and said, 'But it only took you 30 seconds to do it.' Picasso laughed, 'But it has taken me 30 years to be able to do it in 30 seconds.'

Like Picasso, the people who seem to be able effortlessly to change their careers, lives, workplaces, change minds, change the status quo, are people who have spent years learning how to do it. And the aim of this book is to deliver to you a fast-track guide to how they do it, so you can too.

I have researched and interviewed hundreds of the most productive people and teams in the world, who all have a carefully trained capacity for creating change, both in themselves and others. What I learned is distilled here.

The great news is that this ability to make things happen is a skill that you can develop, and the even better news is that, unlike Picasso, it will not take you 30 years to get there (unless you are a really slow reader). In this book, I will show you the practical techniques of the change catalysts: those who know how to make change happen. Start using your new-found change powers and you'll discover the thrill of being able to change anything you like, however entrenched or seemingly impossible.

The principles are the same whether you want to change your life, change your workplace, improve your relationships, drop a bad habit, boost your confidence, get rid of

blocks to progress or become a one-man (or one-woman) powerhouse at work. So whatever it is that you want to change, it all starts right here.

What follows may surprise you. It certainly will if you expect successful change to be all about plans and processes, schedules and logistics. Because it isn't. The root of all successful change is that which tackles the very essence of being human – our drives, our beliefs, our thought processes; ours and those of others. Understand *why* you do what you've always done, and why others have done what they've always done, and immediately you start down the road to successful change.

The curse of knowledge

"It is not when you hit the drum. It's when you *don't* that really makes the difference.**"**

Ringo Starr

I know that you can learn to change absolutely anything you want to. Whether it's your mood, a difficult situation, other people's opinions, bad relationships, an unsatisfying career – whatever it is, you can change it. I know you can. The tricky bit is showing you how in a way that will make it as quick, as simple and as entertaining to grasp as is humanly possible. It's tricky because I'm the tapper and you're the listener.

Let me explain.

Psychology graduates at Stanford University studied a simple game in which people were assigned to one of two roles: 'tappers' or 'listeners'. Tappers received a list of 25 well-known songs, such as *Happy Birthday To You* and *Yankee Doodle Dandy*. Each tapper was asked to pick a song and tap out the rhythm to the listener (by knocking on a table). The listener's job was to guess the song, based on the rhythm being tapped. (Try this same experiment at home.)

The listener's job in this game is quite difficult. Over the course of the experiment, 120 songs were tapped out. Listeners guessed only 2.5 per cent of the songs: 3 out of 120.

But here's what makes the result worthy of your attention. Before the listeners guessed the name of the song, the tappers were asked to predict the percentage of songs that the listeners would guess correctly. They predicted 50 per cent.

The tappers actually got the song across just one time in forty, but they thought they were getting it across one time in two. Why?

When a tapper taps, they hear the song in their head. Go ahead and try it for yourself – tap out *Happy Birthday To You*. It's impossible to avoid hearing the tune in your head. Meanwhile, the listeners can't hear that tune – all they can hear is a bunch of disconnected taps, like a bizarre Morse code.

In the experiment, tappers are flabbergasted at how hard the listener seems to be working to pick up the tune. *Isn't the song obvious?* The tapper's expressions, when a listener guesses *Yankee Doodle Dandy* instead of *Happy Birthday To You*, are priceless. The phrase, 'How could you be so stupid?' is written across their face.

It's hard to be a tapper. The problem is that tappers have been given knowledge (the song title) that makes it impossible for them to imagine what it's like to *lack* that knowledge. When they're tapping they can't imagine what it's like for the listeners to hear isolated taps rather than a song. This is the *curse of knowledge*. Once we know something, we find it hard to imagine what it was like not to know it. Our knowledge has 'cursed' us. And it becomes difficult for us to share our knowledge with others, because we can't readily recreate our listener's state of mind.

This is important for making change happen as it shows very clearly that what you think you are communicating can be a far stretch from what others are actually taking on board. But it's also important here because the tapper/listener experiment is re-enacted every time anyone picks up a book. This time, I am the tapper and you are the listener. As above, we both suffer from an enormous information imbalance. So how can we overcome this?

It's a problem that's hard to avoid. Reversing the process is as impossible as un-ringing a bell. You can't unlearn what you already know. There are, in fact, only two ways to beat the curse of knowledge reliably. The first way is down to you and the second way is my responsibility.

Your job as a listener is to read this book with an open mind. If you are going to gain the most value from it and understand how to create change, you need that open mind. Try not to prejudge. Don't dismiss anything without trying it first – and by trying I mean giving it your absolute best shot.

My job is to take what I know about the art and science of creating change and present it to you in a clear way. So, let's start tapping…

Let's start at the very beginning

First, you need to decide what it is that you want to change. It needs to be as specific as possible. Even if you think you know what it is, don't skip this section as it's crucially important that you are as clear as you can be on exactly what you want to change and have clarified in your mind exactly the point you're starting from.

So, think about the area of your life where you know things aren't what they could be and change is needed. This could be your health, family, career, hobbies, friends or finances. It's your choice. If you have several areas that qualify as 'in need of attention', pick one to start on. When you have chosen, write it down.

Now give yourself an honest mark out of ten for that area, in terms of how satisfied you are with that part of your life.

Why do we need to do this? It is a crucial part of making change happen.

Too often, when we set off to make things better, we can be beset by what psychologists call change blindness. There is a 30-second film made by Harvard psychologists which emphasises this point. The film features six basketball players; three of them are wearing white T-shirts while the other three are wearing black T-shirts. The people in white shirts have a basketball and, during the film, pass it between one another. Halfway through, a man dressed as a gorilla slowly walks on to the court, saunters through the players, beats his chest in front of the camera and then walks off.

Volunteers are asked to watch the film and count the number of times the people in white T-shirts pass the basketball to one another. At the end of the film, when everyone is asked whether they saw anything unusual, amazingly about 80 per cent of the viewers have failed to spot the gorilla. This is the perfect demonstration of the psychological blind spot that we all have.

The singer Ian Brown suggests that 'it doesn't matter where you're from, it's where you're at' that really counts, but I'd like to differ with the Stone Roses frontman. **When you start to implement the ideas and begin making change happen, you too may not notice initially exactly where you started from, but if you can remember, it makes it clear how far you have come.**

Imagine standing at the stretch of a railway line with two parallel rails running off to a distant horizon. Then imagine if you were to unbolt one of the rails and set it just one degree away from parallel. The difference would be barely noticeable from where you're standing now, but 50 miles down the track those rails would be nearly a mile apart. With some similar tiny variations, you can also generate significant change in your life.

I would like you to keep this part of your life, the part you'd like to change for the better, in mind as you read this book. It may be a relationship, it may be your career direction, it doesn't matter. Choose it and keep it in mind as we go through the ten steps of creating change, and understand how by making small changes you too can achieve significantly improved results.

Step

1

'Behaviour is a mirror in which everyone displays his own image.'

Johann Wolfgang von Goethe

Create the right first impression: approaching change in a way that makes the journey smoother

A man is sitting at a bar in an airport when he notices a beautiful woman alongside him. 'Wow,' he thinks, 'she must be an air hostess. I wonder which airline she works for.' He leans over and utters the Delta Airlines slogan, 'Love to fly and it shows.' She gives him a blank stare and he thinks, 'Hmmm. Not Delta.'

Another slogan pops into his head and he leans over again: 'Something special in the air'? She gives him another confused look and he scratches American Airlines off his list.

Thinking, 'Perhaps she works for Thai Airways...' he asks, 'Smooth as silk?' This time the woman gets angry, turns to him and says, 'What the f*** do you want?'

The man slumps back in his chair. 'Ahhh, a budget airline,' he sighs.

This joke got me thinking about the power of first impressions and the speed at which we reach them. How long do you think it takes you to make up your mind about someone you meet for the very first time? A whole second? Two seconds? Ten?

"How long do you think it takes you to make up your mind about someone you meet for the very first time?"

First impressions: 'You had me at hello'

Have you ever seen the film *Jerry Maguire*? There's a brilliant scene towards the end of the film when Tom Cruise visits his ex-girlfriend's house, wanting to win her back. He finds the house full of women all complaining about men so he launches into a long speech, explaining how much he loves her. She interrupts him halfway through and says, 'Stop right now. You had me at hello.'

The part of our brain that leaps to these immediate conclusions is called the adaptive unconscious and the study of this kind of decision-making is one of the most important new fields in psychology. The adaptive unconscious is like a kind of giant computer that quickly processes a lot of data that we need in order to function as human beings.

When you walk out into the street and suddenly realise that a truck is bearing down on you, do you have time to think through all of your options? Of course not. The only way that human beings have survived as a species is that we've developed another kind of decision-making apparatus that's capable of making very quick judgements. As the psychologist Timothy D. Wilson writes in his book *Strangers to Ourselves*, 'The adaptive unconscious does an excellent job of sizing up the world, warning people of danger, setting goals and initiating action in a sophisticated and efficient manner.'

Wilson suggests that we switch back and forth between our conscious and unconscious modes of thinking, depending on the situation. A decision to invite someone to dinner is conscious. You think it over. You decide it will be fun. You ask. However, the spontaneous decision to argue with that same person is made unconsciously – by a different part of your brain. Whenever we meet someone for the first time, whenever we interview someone for a job, whenever we react to a new idea, whenever we're faced with making a decision quickly, we use that second – unconscious – part of our brain.

How long, for example, did it take you to decide how good your teachers were at school? A class? Two classes? A term? The Harvard psychologist Nalini Ambady once gave students three ten-second videotapes of a teacher – with the sound turned off – and found that they had no difficulty rating the teacher's effectiveness. Then the clips were cut back to five seconds and the ratings were the same. They were remarkably consistent even when the students were shown just two seconds of videotape. When these scores were compared with the evaluations made by the teacher's students after a full term of classes, they were essentially the same.

In other words, a person watching a silent two-second clip of a teacher they have never met will typically reach the same conclusions as a student who has sat in the teacher's class for an entire term. That's the power of our adaptive unconscious.

This same adaptive unconscious has also been tested with politicians standing for election to the US Senate. In research conducted at Princeton University, student volunteers were presented with pairs of black and white photographs containing headshots of the winners and runners-up for the US Senate in 2000, 2002 and 2004. From each pair of photographs, the students were asked to choose which of the pair looked more competent. Even though the students saw the pairs of photographs for just one second, choosing which of the two looked most competent mirrored the actual election results about 70 per cent of the time.

Think about your own judgements. Can you honestly recall the words from a speech made by a current political leader? Do you have an opinion about that same leader's effectiveness? Exactly.

It is safe to assume that we make instant judgements about others within the first 30 seconds.

So, what's this got to do with you making change happen?

Two things. And two very important things at that.

First, it's very possible that you are making instant judgements about a lot of things. Some of these might be helpful (such as a truck bearing down on you), but some might not (your opinion that everybody in your company's IT department is useless). If you start to question whether you've jumped to a conclusion – 'why do I think that?' – you start to open up the possibility for change. These snap judgements and instant impressions aren't always correct.

And, secondly, other people are clearly making instant judgements about you. Chances are it would really help you, in whatever you want to make happen, if you could change how you are perceived by others. Whether this is the way your partner sees you, or your boss or colleagues, or a new potential contact. If you want to change how you are perceived at home or at work or wherever, you need to be aware and conscious that others will judge you very quickly. So creating the best impression possible at the outset will pay dividends later. This principle applies just as much to longstanding relationships as when meeting people for the first time. You can always change the way people 'see' you. You just need to know how.

"You can always change the way people 'see' you. You just need to know how."

Goose thinking

By taking the time to make the right first impression, the positive judgements will have a long-term significance. In order to explain why, we need to understand how we think more like baby geese than you may imagine.

A few decades ago, the naturalist Konrad Lorenz discovered that goslings, upon breaking out of their eggs, become attached to the first moving object they encounter (which is generally their mother). Lorenz knew this because in one

experiment *he* became the first thing they saw, and they followed him loyally from then on, demonstrating not only that goslings make initial decisions on first impressions but also that they stick with these decisions once made. Lorenz called this natural phenomenon *imprinting*.

Is the human brain wired like that of a gosling? Do first impressions and decisions also become imprinted? And, if so, how does this imprinting play out in our lives? You can try answering these important questions with a couple of simple experiments.

First, find a volunteer and ask them the following questions:

Question 1: *Is the Mississippi River longer or shorter than 5000 miles?*

Question 2: *How long is the Mississippi?*

When I ask these questions, the majority of people say (correctly) that the Mississippi is shorter than 5000 miles, and when asked for the actual length, most of them give estimates in the 3500-mile range.

Now find a different volunteer and present a slightly different pair of questions:

Question 1: *Is the Mississippi River longer or shorter than 500 miles?*

Question 2: *How long is the Mississippi?*

Again, nearly everyone will get the answer to the first question right – they will say the river is longer than 500 miles. Question 2 is exactly the same as the second question in the first pair, but the answers are usually vastly different, averaging in the 1500-mile range.

What's happening here?

It turns out that people use the information from the first question to anchor their estimates for the second question, even though most of them know the answer to the first is way off. The actual answer is 2320 miles.

For further evidence of how powerful the anchoring effect is, try this next exercise with two groups of friends. Give each group a multiplication problem, but instead of calculating the answer, give them two or three seconds to make a rough estimate:

Group 1: *What is the product of 1 × 2 × 3 × 4 × 5 × 6 × 7 × 8?*

Group 2: *What is the product of 8 × 7 × 6 × 5 × 4 × 3 × 2 × 1?*

If we put these questions side by side, the numbers are the same, so if we are truly logical beings our answer should be the same for both. However, we're psychological beings – without the pure logic or vast processing power of a computer – so we take shortcuts.

When I ask people to answer the first question by itself, the answer averages about 500. But when I reverse the order of the numbers, the answer averages well above 2000, more than four times higher. Here again, people estimate by calculating the product of the first few numbers and then projecting the total from there. In reality, most people vastly underestimate the correct answer, which is 40,320.

What is the point of this?

Well, it shows that what's good for the goose is good for humans as well. In academic lingo, this is called anchoring and it plays a big part in understanding how our goose-like imprinting helps form impressions of other people.

"Anchoring plays a big part in understanding how our goose-like imprinting helps form impressions of other people."

In an experiment similar to the multiplication problems above, Solomon Asch, one of the pioneers of social psychology, gave participants six-word descriptions of the behaviour of people. The words were *intelligent, industrious, impulsive, critical, stubborn* and *envious*. He then asked people to write a broader description of those people on the basis of the six words.

As you can see, Asch included both negative and positive words. But for one group of participants he presented the positive words first; for the other he reversed the order. For both groups, the words were exactly the same.

Yet Asch found a striking difference in how the participants characterised the person they were describing, depending on whether the first words they encountered were positive or negative. Here are some excerpts from the responses of participants who were given the positive words first (that is, *intelligent, industrious, impulsive, critical, stubborn, envious*):

A person who knows what he wants and goes after it. He is impatient [sic] at people who are less gifted, and ambitious with those who stand in his way.

Is a forceful person, has his own convictions and is usually right about things.

> *The person is intelligent and fortunately puts his intelligence to work. That he is stubborn and impulsive may be due to the fact that he knows what he is saying and what he means and will not therefore give in easily to someone else's idea which he disagrees with.*

The participants who heard the negative words before the positive terms had a significantly different take on the imagined person:

> *This person's good qualities such as industry and intelligence are bound to be restricted by jealousy and stubbornness. The person is emotional. He is unsuccessful because he is weak and allows his bad points to cover up his good ones.*

> *This individual is probably maladjusted because he is envious and impulsive.*

Just changing the order of the words was enough to drastically alter the participants' first impressions. The first word anchored the description and coloured how they interpreted the rest of them. So let's relate this understanding to how we make change happen.

If you were to consciously think about the first impression you make on others, accentuating the behaviours you want them to remember you by, it allows you to enjoy basking in the warms rays that a positive impression casts over your future encounters with them. For example, appearing enthusiastic when meeting a new customer will create a powerful memory that will be conjured up the next time they meet you. When they anticipate meeting you for the second occasion, they will immediately remember the bounce and passion you showed and start to become positively disposed before you even arrive.

'This is fine,' you may think, 'when meeting someone for the very first time. But what about existing relationships? How do I change impressions that have already been formed?'

Read on.

Step

2

'I acted like a superstar long before I ever was one.'

Noel Gallagher

Decide how you want to be perceived: using what you say and do to win over others

It is possible to change the way that we are perceived by people we have known for a while, even our partners or our colleagues. To achieve this, take a second to think about meeting someone for the first time. What do you base your instant judgements on?

The magic numbers

Back in the 1960s, Dr Albert Mehrabian, a professor at University College of Los Angeles, provided us with some fascinating research which is continually cited whenever the subject of body language is discussed. He gave us the magic digits: 55, 38 and 7.

He found that first impressions are based on three elements of communication: 55 per cent visual (non-verbal), 38 per cent vocal (such things as tone of voice, rhythm and inflection) and 7 per cent verbal (meaning the actual words used).

So, in a face-to-face encounter:

- 93 per cent of the impact of your message is non-verbal (55 per cent what others see, 38 per cent how you sound).
- 7 per cent of the impact of your message is verbal (the words: what and how you say them).

Put simply, this tells us that most communication in any interaction with another person (face to face) is delivered through body signals or behaviour.

"Most communication in any interaction with another person is delivered through body signals or behaviour."

So, if you think about what you are taking in when you form a first impression of somebody, it's likely to include dress sense, body language, tone of voice and accent – in other words, factors that fit within the 93 per cent non-verbal category. It is our behaviour: the things we say and the things we do. It is our body language, the way we speak, the way we dress, the way we laugh. It is how we respond to different situations. The things we can do; the things we can't do – all of which are shown by the way we act and the way we behave.

Think back to the start of this book and the segment of your life you most want to change. Write down four or five words that you would use to describe your behaviour when you are at your absolute 100 per cent best in that situation. If I was watching you, what behaviours would I see? What would you be saying and doing?

Self-consistency theory

In the classic movie *The Greatest Story Ever Told*, legendary cowboy action hero John Wayne was famously miscast as a Roman centurion.

Wayne's pivotal line, spoken while looking at Christ's body nailed to the cross – 'but he truly is the son of God' – was apparently not being delivered with quite the gusto John Huston, the director, had envisioned. 'It needs more awe,' directed Huston and then stood back to capture the scene.

John Wayne stepped forward, squinted at the figure on the cross and drawled the line, 'Awww…he truly is the son of Gawwd.'

I love this story because it captures a great example of an important psychological concept known as the self-consistency theory and is the reason why writing down your best behaviours is so important.

Prescott Lecky, one of the pioneers of this self-image psychology, believed that humans have an inherent need for consistency. If a thought is inconsistent with other stronger ideas and concepts, the mind will reject it. In John Wayne's case, his self-image of being the heroic cowboy of Western epics was far stronger than the idea of himself as a Roman soldier.

More seriously, an example of how this works is illustrated by the mental illness anorexia. If a sufferer regards themselves as being overweight, despite the obvious evidence to the contrary in a mirror, they will only see an overweight reflection staring back, prompting them to continue their destructive weight-loss behaviours. The self-consistency theory means that we act according to the image we hold of ourselves.

"The self-consistency theory means that we act according to the image we hold of ourselves."

A long time ago in a galaxy far, far away, Luke Skywalker's character understood this same principle and used it to persuade Darth Vader to turn against the evil emperor, saving his own life and restoring hope and peace to the galaxy. How did he use the self-consistency theory to secure this compliance, and what lessons does it offer to help you identify your own best behaviours when creating change?

In the movie *Return of the Jedi*, the final episode of the *Star Wars* series, there is a scene in which Luke Skywalker turns to Darth Vader and says, 'I know there is still good in you. There's good in you, I can sense it.' It was these simple words that persuaded Vader – or at least planted the seeds of persuasion – to look at his behaviour and come away from the Dark Side. When we understand the self-consistency theory, Luke Skywalker's successful tactic appears obvious.

When we assign a behaviour or characteristic to a person or even to ourselves, and then make a request that is consistent with that behaviour, we will naturally strive to demonstrate it.

For example, research has shown how it could be used to increase the likelihood that people would vote on an election day. Researchers interviewed a large number of potential voters and randomly told half of them that, based on their responses, they could be characterised as 'above-average citizens likely to vote and participate in political events'. The other half of the interviewees were informed that they could be characterised as about average in terms of their likelihood to vote.

Those respondents labelled as being good citizens and having a high likelihood of voting not only came to see themselves as better citizens than those labelled as average, but they were also 15 per cent more likely to vote in an election held one week later.

Of course, this technique isn't limited to political domains or attempts to depose an intergalactic emperor. There are a number of ways in which you can use this technique to help yourself create change in your life too, even in situations when you have longstanding relationships with others.

Using the self-consistency theory is the easiest step to achieve our own strong self-image. In fact, you will already have applied it on at least two separate occasions in your life. Let's look at them in turn.

"Using the self-consistency theory is the easiest step to achieve our own strong self-image."

CV

When you apply for a job and complete your CV or application form, you will identify and then write down your best behaviours, such as 'I am an enthusiastic team player', and then you will do your best to demonstrate these same behaviours in the interview.

This was the reason why Rudolph Giuliani placed such emphasis on his employees' CVs when he was Mayor of New York City. He insisted that they updated and completed their résumé every year and present it to him. This was the basis on which he agreed to allow people to continue working in his team. Giuliani understood that when we complete such a task, it is one of the few occasions when we take the time to apply the self-consistency theory and identify our own best behaviours.

There is an old joke about a man being interviewed for a new job and being told, 'In this job we really need someone who is responsible.' The man thinks for a moment and then replies, 'I am perfect for you. In my last job, lots of things went badly wrong and they always said I was responsible.'

Can you imagine if you were also completely honest and wrote your typical, everyday behaviours? Writing information like, 'I am not good on a Monday morning' or 'I tend to wind down on a Friday afternoon' or 'I am particularly skilled at complaining about my boss'? If you adopted this approach, you'd be unlikely to get past the rubbish bin stage of the recruitment process. Giuliani noted, 'When you get people to identify their best behaviours, they will naturally start to try and live up to them.'

Why not write your own annual CV – for work and life – and identify who you are when you are at your very best? If you are a leader, could you get your team to do something similar?

First date

Billy Connolly sometimes jokes about spotting the danger signs of complacency creeping into his relationship with his wife. He suggests that when he wrote the message on his wife's Valentine card, 'I love you, dear. PS See last year's card for details', he knew there was trouble ahead!

This joke reminds me of the other likely occasion when you are clear about your best behaviours and then strive to live up to them.

Cast your mind back to your very first date with your current partner. You will have been keen to make a good impression and so gave serious thought to your best behaviours and how to demonstrate them. You will have looked your best, been attentive, funny, charming and charismatic, right? Now think about your average behaviours today. How far are you from that first impression? Is that where you need to move towards to bring about the change that is important to you?

Four-minute rule

As we discussed, first impressions are the ones that will have the greatest impact on others, no matter how much time you spend with them. In these initial minutes, we quickly judge a person and this judgement is the one that tends to stick. This principle resulted in O.J. Simpson employing eight – yes, eight – behavioural consultants to advise him on his behaviour, his clothes and his general appearance when he first appeared in court charged with murder.

He knew that the jurors would be making snap decisions about him based on his initial appearance and that these judgements would remain the same despite the evidence presented to them.

I have a personal example of the potential power of using these minutes effectively. A friend regularly works away from home and was explaining to me how he used to be too tired to enjoy spending time with his young family, resulting in fractious and short-tempered weekends.

When he stopped to analyse his own behaviour, he realised that he was not helping himself. When he parked the car in the drive, he immediately carried his bags, his suitcase and his coat into the house with him, weighing him down like a packhorse. When his three children ran to greet him, his first words were, 'Give me a minute. Let me get in the door.' This would cause his youngest child to flee to his mother in tears. He would listen distractedly as the others described their week.

He would then locate his wife, comforting a crying toddler, and the first words from her mouth were, 'I can see that you're home again.'

Nowadays, using the self-consistency theory to his advantage, he takes a moment before entering the house to think about how the best father and husband would behave. Being clear about this has led to some subtle behavioural changes and some powerful results.

He now leaves his bags and coat in the car so he is unencumbered. After he turns the door key in the lock, his immediate action is to hold out his arms, ready to greet his children who rush to see him. He carries his three sons to wherever his wife is, and he describes the hug they enjoy as his 'Disney' moment.

The impact of these first few moments is seismic. After embracing his family and behaving like 'the best dad in the world' for the first four minutes, he has created a powerful first impression. He claims that after this effort, he can go back to behaving like a miserable sod but nobody notices!

In reality, they perceive him in such a positive light that he is more inclined to want to live up to these expectations, creating a virtuous circle. Psychologists often dub this the 'Matthew effect', after the lines in the Gospel of St Mark 25:29, which state, 'To everyone who has, will more be given, and he will have abundance. But from him who has not, even what he has will be taken away.'

It may sound like heavenly stuff, but it is merely another way of saying that we get more of what we give. It is just the same for us and our behaviour when creating change.

Change action

When Sir Clive Woodward was the coach of the England rugby union team, he thought deeply about his own behaviours, especially at crucial moments such as during his half-time team talks.

He called it 'second half thinking' and used the ten-minute break to influence the thinking of his players. Rather than worrying about whether they were winning or losing after the first half, he insisted on his players changing their shirts and wearing a new kit while he would think about his own behaviour and impact to influence the players. He describes how those crucial ten minutes should be used:

0–2 minutes
Absolute silence
Think about performance
Shirts off
Towel down
New kit
0–0 on scoreboard

2–5 minutes
Coaches' assessments
Take on food and fluids

5–8 minutes
Coach's final word

8–10 minutes
Absolute silence
0–0 on scoreboard
Visualise kick-off

Source: Clive Woodward (2004), *Winning!* London: Hodder & Stoughton.

How many of us have thought (usually after a day or moment or event has gone disastrously wrong), 'If only I could rewind and do that again'? This is a way of doing just that, even when something is halfway through. It's not too late. In the above example, the team is effectively getting the chance to start again halfway through the match. They wipe clean what's happened and focus on the way they want things to be in the next half.

This is a way of making sure tomorrow is better than today and that you're not repeating the same mistakes over and over.

So why not do a similar breakdown for the first few minutes of your own day, or the first few minutes of a meeting, or the first few minutes of a conversation and focus on the change-creating behaviours which you want to demonstrate to others? Use the following table to list these behaviours.

1–2 minutes
Behaviour:

2–3 minutes
Behaviour:

3–4 minutes
Behaviour:

Mirror, mirror on the wall...

You could also consider adopting a really simple technique of writing these desired behaviours in a place where you will see them on a daily basis – for example, the mirror you use to check your appearance before leaving the house.

I know this seems slightly bizarre as no one doubts that the primary purpose of a mirror is to see what we look like on the outside, but the mirror could also act as a window into what we look like on the inside – and perhaps, more importantly, how we *want* to look and behave.

"The mirror could act as a window into what we look like on the inside."

This was the basis for a fantastic psychological study conducted one Hallowe'en. Researchers temporarily converted 18 local houses into makeshift research facilities and, when trick-or-treaters rang the doorbell of one of the houses, a research assistant greeted them, asked their names and then pointed to a large bowl of sweets on a nearby table. After telling the children that they could each take just *one* of the sweets, she mentioned that she had some work to do and quickly left the room.

That was the treat part of the experiment. And here's the trick: what the children didn't know, besides the fact that they were in a cleverly devised experiment, was that someone was watching them through a hidden camera. That person was another research assistant who had the job of recording whether each child behaved dishonestly by taking more than one sweet.

When the results came in, the data revealed that 35 per cent of the kids took more than they should have. But the researchers wanted to see whether they could reduce the rate of theft through the use of a mirror.

In these cases, before the bell rang, the research assistant angled a large mirror by the bowl of sweets in such a way that the trick-or-treaters had to look at themselves in the mirror when they took the sweets. The theft rate with the mirror? Only 8.9 per cent.

I used this same approach with one retail organisation and adapted the dress code so that all employees were required to wear a tie as part of their uniform. A mirror, with the perfect employee behaviours on it, was also distributed to all stores.

Staff had to use the mirror to put the tie on correctly and so, when they checked their appearance, they were subconsciously reminded of the required behaviours. Within the first 12 months, an improvement in their execution had been recorded and customer feedback also improved. Significantly, the profits rose too.

Where could you remind yourself of how you want to behave on a regular basis to help bring about the desired change in your life?

Change action

Analyse your daily routine and identify three potential points where you could remind yourself of your best behaviours.

This simple task acts as a good trigger to help you refocus on the things that matter. It can be small notes stuck on frequently used things, like phones and computer screens. These reminders act as a trigger to recognise how you are behaving and whether that's different from how you want to behave. One friend changes the names of difficult customers on her mobile phone to instructions on how to behave. For example, if she speaks to a demanding client, the command 'Stand tall and speak confidently' indicates his phone call and offers a quick prompt before she answers.

▶

If you're trying to change the way you behave – to be more confident or more thoughtful, for example – it might be that this is a short-term step until the way you want to behave has become so ingrained that you don't need reminding.

This said, all of us need a reminder sometimes. When a couple I know got married, one of the wedding presents they received was a beautifully handwritten extract from the book *Rules of Love* – entitled 'Be Nice'. The couple put it on their kitchen wall. We're talking about one of the most thoughtful, supportive, generally lovely couples you can imagine, and yet even they admit to checking and amending their behaviour towards each other when they happen to glance at it.

Behaviour drives performance: teamwork

So far these ideas have related mainly to individuals, but how do you use the self-consistency theory with a group wanting to make changes?

Perhaps the most visible example of the kind of focused physical and mental energy which all teams look for is found in professional sport, where high levels of focus and concentration are the norm. At the top level, all participants have the physical attributes, skills and abilities of champions. The consistent winners, however, focus all their energies on the behaviours that lead to their goal and stop the behaviours that get in the way.

"Consistent winners focus all their energies on the behaviours that lead to their goal."

One of the tasks I like to ask sports coaches to do is to describe the perfect game. Great coaches will quickly and easily outline the physical, tactical and technical aspects they consider essential. The best coaches will, however, then extend their description to include the winning behaviours on display. These are coaches who have often witnessed games where the difference has been the superior behaviours of the winning team.

Although no game is ever perfect, this exercise is useful because it considers the end point of their work and allows a discussion about how a perfect coach would react to the many challenging situations that can occur. Dr Ric Charlesworth, the legendary coach of the Australian women's double Olympic gold medallist hockey team, the Hockeyroos, would do this. He would get his players to work through hypothetical situations in groups and describe how the perfect player and the perfect coach would behave.

Sir Alex Ferguson also champions this approach, suggesting that there are *mechanics* and *dynamics* of a team – or, as others have described them, the physics and the chemistry. He believes that as well as the rigorous skills training which players receive, working on the dynamics or behaviour of a team is equally important.

WOPAS

I promised one leading sports team I was working with that they would change and improve their performance as long as they were prepared to be honest about each other's behaviour as elite players. Behaviour and personality are different factors (less than 10 per cent of behaviour is down to personality) and so, unlike the technical assessment of skills and abilities these guys had been subjected to repeatedly as players, they had rarely ever discussed the best behaviours. This time we sat in a circle and openly and honestly agreed upon the five behaviours that consistently brought them the best results.

We then adapted an idea which Jeff Bezos, the CEO of Amazon, implemented with his customer service staff. He set up WOCAS (What Our Customers Are Saying) reports, which went straight to him, along with 'customer verbatim' – the actual emails sent in by customers – on the behaviours which they felt were most important.

In our sports team, our approach was to create a WOPAS (What Our Peers Are Saying) report, with everyone on the team assessing each other's behaviour after every game.

There was a particular example that highlighted the power of this simple system. The team captain had driven his team mercilessly during training. In his mind, he had done what was required of him because they had fully completed the training exercise on time. And using the traditional assessment guidelines, the boxes would have been ticked off and that would have been the end of it.

But when we sat down afterwards to look at how he might improve his behaviour and performance he received some very strident feedback from the group, who were in reality using a far more comprehensive set of performance criteria than any technical checklist could provide.

Their feedback suggested that his leadership style was in fact deeply flawed; he'd given no thought whatsoever to the quality of performance, how tired they were by the end of it or how that affected their capacity to train effectively the next day. As obvious as his behavioural shortcomings were once they had been raised, they certainly weren't obvious until the team had pointed them out.

The feedback from the group was extraordinarily positive; their responses unequivocally supported my belief that regular peer feedback (WOPAS reports) on our behaviour amounts to a very powerful learning tool. More profoundly, they concluded that the process had fundamentally changed the way they dealt with each other. Sir Clive Woodward once suggested that 'culture is what happens when you [the leader] are not there'. This process addresses that same concern. Who better to create a winning environment than the people who are responsible?

"Regular peer feedback on our behaviour amounts to a very powerful learning tool."

Other examples of groups that have identified their best behaviours and then assessed themselves regularly against them include Pearson, the global learning giant, which encourages all employees to be 'brave, imaginative and decent'.

Harley-Davidson believes that all its staff should:

- tell the truth
- be fair
- keep their promises
- respect the individual
- encourage intellectual curiosity.

These are all observable and measurable behaviours. It is easy to recognise when individuals are exhibiting truthful behaviour, behaving fairly, keeping promises, showing respect for people and doing things that encourage intellectual curiosity.

At Southwest Airlines, CEO Herb Kelleher asked his staff, 'From the minute you think of working here to the minute you leave, what behaviours will you show that makes this experience unique and separates us from the competition?' His workforce then identified their own 'eight freedoms' (behaviours that defined their working experience at the airline) from 'freedom to work hard and have fun' to 'freedom to create and innovate'.

They spell out what are acceptable and unacceptable behaviours and allow people to be clear about where they need to change.

Do you need to change the behaviours of a group to make the desired change in your life? Maybe your friends, family or work colleagues would benefit from agreeing a code of conduct. It doesn't need to be overtly formal or official. Instead, try sitting them down and asking, 'What do we do as a group that makes us all productive and happy? Can we agree to try to do those things more frequently?'

Behaviour really matters, but it's just the starting point to create change. To consistently be successful in making things happen, we must look at our emotions.

Step

3

'Don't address their brains. Address their hearts.'

Nelson Mandela

Recognise the power of emotions: avoiding the emotional triggers that may jeopardise change

Mother Teresa once said, 'If I look at the mass, I will never act. If I look at the one, I will.' In a recent study, researchers decided to see whether most people think like Mother Teresa when they want to create change.

Researchers wanted to see how people would respond to an opportunity to make charitable donations to a cause as opposed to making a charitable donation to a single person. They used two different request letters. The first version featured statistics about the magnitude of problems facing children in Africa, such as the following:

- *Food shortages in Malawi affect more than three million children.*

- *Four million Angolans – a third of the population – have been forced to flee their homes.*

- *More than 11 million people in Ethiopia need immediate food assistance.*

The other version of the letter gave information about a single young girl:

Any money you donate will go to Rokia, a seven-year-old girl from Mali. Rokia is desperately poor and faces the threat of severe hunger or even starvation. Her life will be changed for the better as a result of your financial gift. With your support, Save the Children will work with Rokia's family and other members of the community to help feed and educate her and provide basic medical care and hygiene education.

The researchers then gave participants one of the two different letters and looked at how much money they wanted to contribute.

On average, the people who read about Rokia contributed twice as much as those who read the statistics. It seems that most people have something in common with Mother Teresa: when it comes to our heart, one individual trumps the masses.

To prove this argument, they ran a second study. In this, they asked people to think in an analytical way by asking them questions such as, 'If an object travels at five feet per minute, then by your calculations how many feet will it travel in 360 seconds?' Other people were primed to think in terms of feelings: 'Please write down one word to describe how you feel when you hear the word "baby".'

Both groups were then given the Rokia letter and, as you can probably guess, the analytically primed people gave less than the people who were primed to feel before they read about Rokia. Researchers dubbed this the 'drop in the ocean effect', after Mother Teresa's famous words: 'We ourselves feel that what we are doing is just a drop in the ocean. But the ocean would be less because of that missing drop.'

The neurologist Donald Calne sums up the lesson we can learn from this when creating change in our own lives: 'The essential difference between emotion and reason is that emotion leads to action while reason leads to conclusions.' This is a profoundly important point. As human beings, we move and create change when our feelings and emotions are touched.

"As human beings, we move and create change when our feelings and emotions are touched."

This point was illustrated in *The Heart of Change* by John Kotter and Dan Cohen, who interviewed over 400 people across the United States, Europe, Australia and South Africa in the hope of understanding why change happens. Summarising the data, Kotter and Cohen said that in most change situations people initially focus on logical solutions, which leads them to miss the most important issue:

> '[...] the core of the matter is always about changing the behaviour of people, and behaviour change happens in highly successful situations mostly by speaking to people's feelings. This is true even in organisations that are very focused on analysis and quantitative measurement, even among people who think of themselves as smart in an MBA sense. In highly successful change efforts, people find ways to help others see the problems or solutions in ways that influence emotions, not just thoughts.'

Kotter and Cohen say that most people think change happens in this order: ANALYSE–THINK–CHANGE. You analyse a situation, then you think about it and then you make the necessary changes. In a normal environment that might work pretty well, but change situations don't look like that. Because of the uncertainty that change brings, analytical arguments will not overcome the reluctance to shift perspective or habits.

Kotter and Cohen observed that, in almost all successful changes, the sequence of change is not ANALYSE–THINK–CHANGE but rather SEE–FEEL–CHANGE. You're presented with evidence that makes you feel something. It might be a disturbing look at the problem, a hopeful glimpse of the solution or a sobering reflection of your current habits but, regardless, it's something that hits you at the emotional level.

This means that we need to make sure we are engaging how we feel to help us to change, and also that to make change happen through others it's vital that we make sure their emotions are brought into play too. **Whoever you are trying to influence needs to care. They need to feel what you feel.**

The food writer Nigel Slater acknowledged the power of emotions in his memoir *Toast*, detailing his childhood years as remembered through their association with food. In one incredibly moving account, he recalls how his father helped him to deal with the overwhelming grief which engulfed him following his mother's death at the age of nine and how this helped forge a stronger relationship between them.

He recalls that the night after his mum's funeral, he saw two white marshmallows on his bedside table: 'I had never been allowed to eat in bed, and when my father came upstairs to tuck me in, I asked if they were for me. "Of course they are." He said, "I know they're your favourites." He explained how he had read a school essay written shortly before my mother's death, in which I had described them as being the nearest food to a kiss. Each night for the next two years I found two, sometimes three, fluffy, sugary marshmallows waiting for me. It was my mother's goodnight kiss.'

Think back to when you were a kid and wanted to ask your parents for some money or, as an adult, if you wanted to invite someone out on a date. How did you approach the problem? What worked? What didn't?

Most people agree that a simple statement of your intentions has the odds stacked against it, and a demand that your parents hand over the cash or that the lady or gentleman in question gives you their heart or body before even knowing your name is unlikely to yield either financial or romantic satisfaction. In the end, most of us agree that the only way to increase your chance of success is to mentally step out of your shoes and into theirs and figure out their emotional hot buttons.

"The only way to increase your chance of success is to figure out their emotional hot buttons."

'Aha!' moments

Leaders often use this same understanding in order to change people's behaviour to deliver improved results. The New York Police Department (NYPD) transformed itself from being the worst police organisation in America to the best within two years by doing this. William Bratton, the chief of police, had to motivate 35,000 police officers to improve many of their accepted, everyday behaviours.

Bratton could have chosen to wake up his organisation to the need for change by pointing to the unacceptable number of crimes taking place. However, as we have already seen in our behaviours, what we say, including quoting statistics, simply doesn't cut it. They make up just 7 per cent of what we remember. It is what we actually see that matters.

Bratton's first step appeared to be an odd one: he instructed all senior officers to travel to work by subway, banning them from using their cars to commute. This way, the NYPD leaders had to face the problem head-on. When these senior New York police officers had to take the 'electric sewer' instead, they immediately saw the horror that citizens were up against – aggressive beggars, gangs of youths jumping turnstiles, jostling people and drunks sprawled on benches.

With that ugly reality, the officers could no longer deny the urgent need for change in their policing methods and behaviour. Although statistics are disputable and hardly inspiring or memorable, the face-to-face experience was shocking. Bratton recognised the disproportionate influence of people's feelings on their behaviour. Psychologists refer to this as the 'Aha! moment'. It made them start to take action.

Understanding and controlling our own emotional state is therefore an important feature in allowing us the best chance to consistently display our best change-making behaviour.

But let's first look at a common mistake many of us make when doing this.

Feelings versus pre-feelings

We can have a tough time imagining a tomorrow that is terribly different from today and we find it particularly difficult to imagine that we will ever think or feel differently than we do now.

This is why teenagers get tattoos, because they are confident that 'Death rocks' will always be an appealing motto, or smokers who have just finished a cigarette are so confident, for at least five minutes, that they can easily quit and that their resolve will not diminish with the nicotine in their bloodstreams.

Indeed, one of the hallmarks of depression is that when depressed people think about future events, they cannot imagine enjoying them very much. This makes good sense, as they find it difficult to feel happy today and thus find it difficult to believe that they will feel happy tomorrow.

You may be familiar with a less dramatic example of this. Have you ever gone to the supermarket to do your weekly shopping after you have already eaten? Research has demonstrated that when we have recently eaten, trying to decide what we will want to eat next week reliably causes us to underestimate the extent of our future appetites and we end up buying less food than we need. The food does not temporarily lower our intelligence.

Rather, we find it difficult to imagine being hungry when we are feeling full and we can't bring ourselves to properly provide for hunger's inevitable return.

What is true of our stomachs is also true of our minds. In a recent study, some volunteers were asked to answer five quiz questions and were told that after they had taken their best guesses, they would receive one of two rewards:

- Either they would learn the correct answers to the questions and whether they had got them right or wrong.
- Or they would receive a chocolate bar but never get to learn the correct answers.

Some volunteers chose their reward *before* they took the quiz and some chose *after* they took it. As you might expect, people preferred the chocolate bar before taking the quiz but would rather have the answers afterwards.

In other words, taking the quiz had made people so curious that they valued the answers more than a scrumptious piece of chocolate. Beforehand, volunteers who had not actually experienced the intense curiosity that taking the quiz produced simply couldn't imagine feeling that they would refuse the offer of a chocolate bar for a few dull facts.

This finding reminds me of a wonderful scene from the 1967 film *Bedazzled* in which the devil spends his days in bookstores, ripping the final pages out of mystery novels. This may not strike you as an act so utterly evil that it would warrant Lucifer's personal attention, but when you arrive at the end of a good whodunit only to find the whodunit bit missing, you understand why people might willingly trade their mortal souls for the conclusion. Curiosity is a powerful emotion, but when you aren't smack bang in the middle of feeling it, it's hard to imagine just how far and fast it can drive you.

Mixing up our feelings and pre-feelings is one of the world's most common mistakes. In one study, researchers telephoned people in different parts of the country and asked how satisfied they were with their lives. Where the weather was nice, people reported that their lives were relatively happy. But when people lived in cities that happened to have bad weather that day, they reported that they were relatively unhappy.

"Mixing up our feelings and pre-feelings is one of the world's most common mistakes."

These people had tried to answer the question by imagining their lives and then asking themselves how they felt when they did so. Their brains enforced a kind of 'reality first' policy and insisted on reacting to real weather instead of their imaginary lives. A lack of conscious awareness caused them to mistake reality-induced feelings for imagination-induced pre-feelings. Understanding this distinction when creating change is crucial.

You've probably been in a similar conundrum yourself. You've had an awful night's sleep and you wake up feeling out of sorts. You look out of the window and it is raining heavily. If at that moment you try to imagine how much you are looking forward to the working day ahead, you may attribute feelings that are to do with your bad night's sleep to your imaginary day. ('It is going to be terrible.')

In order to achieve our very best behaviours to make change happen on a consistent basis, we must learn to understand this important distinction.

Think about how you would describe yourself when you feel fantastic and outstanding. I'll bet that a number of these words are similar to the words you have written about your best behaviours.

Shortly we'll look at how you can regularly create these feelings to ensure that you are at your best when being a change catalyst. But before we do that, we need to have a quick look at the major obstacle that could prevent this happening.

Stress

If we regularly wake up in the morning feeling sad, down, depressed and tired and then try to force ourselves to produce our best change-making behaviour, what we are doing is putting ourselves under stress. If you are doing this, think how it feels. It isn't fun, is it? More importantly, it isn't good for your health.

So what is stress?

One official definition is: 'The reaction people have to excessive pressures or other types of demands placed on them. It arises when they worry they can't cope.' I prefer the more graphic description: 'Stress is when you wake up screaming and you realise that you haven't fallen asleep yet.'

Hans Seyle, who is a pioneer of modern stress research, says that stress has three components:

- stimulus
- perception
- response.

For example, if we are hiking in the woods and encounter a bear, this is a *stimulus*; we then *perceive* a life-threatening situation and a *response* is activated in our bodies, so we can run for our lives. This important response mechanism has been hard-wired into our genes since the caveman days and is a key survival tool. Let me explain how this works when creating change in more detail.

Our response to the stimulus of change-related stress manifests itself in three ways:

- freeze
- fight
- flight.

You might wonder what this has to do with creating change in the modern world, but if you are either very honest or very observant you will know that it is more than just a metaphorical jungle out there. In this state we will do (or say) whatever it takes to get out of the situation. You cannot reason with people in this state, you cannot build true consensus, you won't hear the truth. You only have access to about 10 per cent of your own and other people's abilities. In other words, **you can't proceed with change (or even with business as normal) unless the freeze, fight or flight mechanism is disarmed.**

Your natural personality will play a part in determining the type of behaviour that you will exhibit when feeling stress about making change happen. Depending on your personality, some people display aggressive behaviour (fight), some people distance themselves from the situation (flight) and some give up and acquiesce to the pressure (freeze).

It also helps if you are able to recognise these responses in others. Common examples include increased absences or a high attrition rate (flight), or even simply where people choose to sit in a room. Remember when you were at school. If you entered a classroom for a lesson you didn't like, where would you sit if possible? At the back? That is the flight response, trying to put as much distance between yourself and the threat, in this case the teacher.

I speak to a lot of leaders who often claim that their biggest frustration when trying to make change happen is people's apparent apathy. 'We do question and answer sessions, suggestion box opportunities and we still get nothing back' is a complaint I have heard numerous times. My answer? That silence is feedback. People normally do have questions and suggestions about how to improve things, but if they are not offering them it suggests that they don't feel safe with you and so are choosing to say nothing (freeze).

Finally, one behaviour I often observe in sporting dressing rooms and among adolescent children, but also unfortunately within business environments, is aggressive, macho posturing or snide, underhanded comments, which is a manifestation of the fight response.

Change action

Consider these potentially stressful situations.

At a meeting for which you have thoroughly prepared, the chair criticises you and accuses you of failing to attend to tasks that were, in reality, someone else's responsibility. As all eyes turn on you, you feel your face getting hot, your jaw tightening and your fist clenching. You would not shout or hit anyone – doing so would only make things worse. But you feel like shouting or striking out.

Now consider another stress-filled scenario. You walk into your weekly evening class a few moments late, only to find everyone putting books and notes away – apparently preparing for a test you did not realise had been scheduled for today. Your heart seems to stop, your mouth is dry, your knees feel weak and you momentarily consider hurrying back out the door. Your life is not really in danger, and running away will not solve your problem – so why should you feel a physical urge to escape?

Finally, imagine walking alone down a dark street. You hear a startling noise. Without thinking, you stop dead in your tracks. Your senses become razor sharp. Your eyes widen and scan the scene, taking in as much visual information as possible. You may even hold your breath in an effort to become completely silent and still, and to hear better. You become 'an alarmed-looking human statue'.

These three scenarios illustrate the **freeze, fight or flight response**, a sequence of internal processes that prepares you for struggle or escape. It is triggered when we interpret a situation as threatening. The resulting response depends on how you have *learned* to deal with threat, as well as on an *innate* freeze, fight or flight 'program' built into the brain.

Don't believe me? I have regularly tested it out with a simple experiment on a number of different groups and audiences, of all ages and experience, where I take £10 out of my pocket, hold it up and ask if anyone wants the money.

▶

You would think that it was a no-brainer, wouldn't you? Who would say no to free money? The outcome is always the same. Silence. Followed by a little more silence, followed by nervous laughter. I even hear people telling their friends to go up and get the money. Eventually someone runs up and grabs the money out of my hand at which point everyone claps and the lucky winner immediately tries to give the money back, even though it was offered to them with no strings attached! There is one reason why I am never trampled by a rush of people coming to grab the money. It is that voice in your head (if you are wondering 'Which voice?', it's that one!) which is shouting, 'It's an evil trick! If I run up there to collect the money everyone will laugh at me. I don't understand the game. It can't be that simple. I will make a fool of myself.' In other words, the freeze response grips many of us.

If you're not sure whether you are prone to fight, freeze or flight, then try to remember (or look out for) the last or next really stressful situation and note what happens. Remember, you're looking to notice the *stimulus* (what happened), the *perception* (how you felt) and the *response* (what you did).

Being aware of – and managing – your own emotions and anticipating, observing and managing the emotional responses of others are crucial to seeing change work. It is our feelings that drive the behaviours that others will judge us on. Failing to do this means that we lose control of our actions and, subsequently, our change results.

Let's now look at the four big needs that will allow us to disarm our natural instincts and retain control of our emotions.

Step

4

'Emotional intelligence is the ability to sense,
understand, and apply the power of emotions as a
source of energy, connection, and influence.'

Barack Obama

Address the four big needs: controlling your feelings to influence change

Emotional factors

A recent UK survey was conducted in which supervisors were asked to rank the importance of ten motivators for their employees. Then they asked the employees to rank the same list in order of what they most wanted from their supervisors. The results were as follows.

Supervisors	Employees
1. Good wages	1. Being valued
2. Job security	2. Feeling in control of things
3. Promotional opportunities	3. Feeling involved
4. Good working conditions	4. Job security
5. Interesting work	5. Good wages
6. Loyalty from management	6. Interesting work
7. Tactful discipline	7. Promotional opportunities
8. Being valued	8. Loyalty from management
9. Feeling involved	9. Good working conditions
10. Feeling in control of things	10. Tactful discipline

Without knowing it, the employees had unwittingly explained that the four most important emotional needs which must be satisfied to prevent stress when making change happen are value, control, belonging and safety. **If any of these factors are missing, stress, or more accurately the flight, fight or freeze response, will be triggered.**

So, let's look at each one of these factors in turn.

Feeling valued

In 1992, Arkansas Governor Bill Clinton was running for the US presidency against President George Bush Senior. A pivotal point in the campaign came on the night of the second nationally televised debate during which the president and his opponent faced questions from a live studio audience.

One woman asked the candidates a rather confusing question: 'How has the national debt affected each of your lives? And if it hasn't, how can you honestly find a cure for the economic problems of the common people if you have no experience in what's ailing them?'

President Bush was in the unenviable position of having to answer first. 'I'm sure it has,' he said, sitting on his stool in the middle of the stage. 'I love my grandchildren. I'm not sure I get the question...well, listen, you oughta be in the White House for a day and hear what I hear...' He struggled for a while longer, talking around the question but never directly addressing it.

Finally, it was Clinton's turn. He got down from his stool, walked towards the woman and said, 'Tell me – how has it affected you again?'

She talked, and for every problem that she raised, he responded with an aspect of his economic plan, phrased in the language and experience of his questioner. Many political commentators believe that, in that moment, Bill Clinton won the American presidency.

It was because he addressed one of our basic emotional needs: he made her feel valued. He involved the woman who asked the question. He didn't talk *at* her, as President Bush had done, but rather talked and engaged *with* her.

Most of us desire the positive emotions brought on by feeling valued. In a recent UK survey, 99 out of 100 people reported that they wanted to be around positive people. These people also reported being more productive when they are around positive people who value them.

"Most of us desire the positive emotions brought on by feeling valued."

One of the first changes that Sir Terry Leahy implemented as Tesco's chief executive was to change the format of a simple question, to dramatic effects. When managers visit a store, they no longer ask, 'What's gone wrong?' but instead spend time looking to praise and value staff and discover what is going right. It is no surprise that Leahy has been voted one of Britain's most admired business leaders.

Change action

Emotional bank account

Jim Thompson is the founder of the Positive Coaching Alliance (PCA), which is on a mission to emphasise that youth sport should not be about winning at all costs; it should be about learning life lessons.

The PCA holds positive-coaching seminars for youth sports coaches. At the seminars, trainers use the analogy of the 'emotional tank' to get coaches to think about the right ratio of praise, support and critical feedback. 'The emotional tank is like the petrol tank of a car. If your car's tank is empty, you can't drive very far. If your emotional tank is empty, you are not going to perform at your best.'

After the emotional tank analogy is introduced, the trainers begin an exercise. First, they ask the coaches to imagine that the person next to them has just missed an important

▶

chance in a game. The coaches are challenged to say some-thing to the person to *drain* their emotional tank. Since clever put-downs are a staple of many sports, the exercise is embraced with noticeable enthusiasm. Thompson says, 'The room fills with laughter as coaches get into the exer-cise, sometimes with great creativity.'

Then the coaches are asked to imagine that someone else has made the same mistake, but they're now in charge of *filling* that person's emotional tank. This generates a more muted response. Thompson says, 'The room often gets very quiet, and you finally hear a feeble, "Nice try!"'

Try the exercise yourself. Think about the change challenge you are working on. Think about how you can fill and drain your own emotional tank (or do the same for someone who is important to your cause). Write down the phrases.

If you're wanting to improve a difficult relationship, take notice of the kinds of things you are saying to that person. Are you being overly critical and hard on them and draining their emotional bank account? Even if you feel negatively towards the person, what happens if you try to notice what they have done right – and comment on it?

If there's somebody who is blocking your efforts to change, are they being difficult because they feel completely unval-ued? How could you help them feel more valued?

Positive focus

Unfortunately, wanting a more positive environment isn't enough. Most of us have grown up in a culture where praise and value is often second to criticism. Although this negativ-ity-based approach might have evolved unintentionally, it nevertheless permeates our society at all levels. Don't believe me? Then tell me, how many times were you ever called in at school to discuss your 'outstanding grades'?

A recent Gallup poll looked at this very issue, in particular parents' focus on their children's best grades compared to the focus on their worst grades.

The survey, carried out across multiple countries and cultures, asked parents the following question: 'Your child shows you the following grades: English – A; Social Studies – A; Biology – C; Algebra – F. Which grade deserves the most attention from you?' The vast majority of parents in every country focused on the F, as shown in the table below.

Country	Focused on As	Focused on Fs
UK	22%	52%
Japan	18%	43%
China	8%	56%
France	7%	87%
US	7%	77%
Canada	6%	83%

I am not suggesting that parents should ignore the F in Algebra. But why not start with a positive focus on the As before working on strategies for improving the F? It could make for a more productive discussion. Equally, when attempting to bring about change in your life, first start by identifying what *is* working before concentrating on what needs to change.

"When attempting to bring about change in your life, first start by identifying what *is* working."

Over 80 years ago, the fields of education and psychology overlooked an important study – one with implications which could have, and probably should have, altered this kind of thinking for ever.

The study, conducted by Dr Elizabeth Hurlock in 1925, was designed to explore what would happen when students in a maths class received different types of feedback on their work. Hurlock wanted to find out if it was more effective to praise, criticise or ignore students. The outcome was to be determined by how many maths problems each student had solved two, three, four and five days after the initial feedback.

Children in the first group were identified by name and praised in front of the class for their good work. Children in the second group were also identified by name in front of the group but were criticised for their poor work. Those in the third group were completely ignored, although they were present to hear the others being praised and scolded. A fourth (control) group was moved to another room after the first test. Members of this group took the same tests, but they received no comments on their performance.

Students in both the praised and criticised groups did better after the first day. Then their performance changed dramatically. The students who were criticised showed a major decline in their test scores and by the third and fourth day, they were performing on a par with students who had been completely ignored.

In contrast, the students who were praised experienced a major improvement after the second day that was sustained through to the end of the study. By the fifth day of this experiment, the group that received praise showed an unequivocally stronger performance than the other study groups. The overall improvement by group was:

Praised – 71 per cent

Criticised – 19 per cent

Ignored – 5 per cent.

Change action

Your strengths represent the things at which you excel. They are the things that you know you can rely on yourself, the attributes and talents that people readily recognise in you. Understanding this will contribute to the sense of value you feel when creating change.

If you find this difficult, then approach your colleagues, family and friends. Talk to them about what they see as your strengths and rate their value. Ask them how you could utilise these strengths more. These conversations will raise your self-awareness and your capacity to focus on your strengths when making things happen. For example, if you are a great listener, could you start to enjoy deeper conversations with the people you need to help create change with?

Similarly, think about how you can apply this same principle of creating value for others.

In the Middle Ages, when lighting a fire from scratch was an arduous process, people would carry about a metal box containing a smouldering cinder, kept alight throughout the day with little bits of kindling. This meant that a man could light a fire with ease wherever he went, because he always carried the spark. You too should aim to offer the 'spark' of positive feedback to others to give them the confidence to face change.

Dr Shad Helmsetter, an American child psychologist, estimates that in the first 16 years of our lives people say no to us about 148,000 times. Get a calculator out and divide 148,000 by 16 and then by 365; it comes to 25 'nos' a day. He also estimates that, on average, parents speak to their children in a negative manner over 90 per cent of the time. No wonder that in related tests, 90 per cent of UK children have a positive self-image at the age of four and yet this figures drops to just 5 per cent by the age of 16.

▶

This continues into our adult lives as well. John Gottman, a psychologist at the University of Washington and someone we will meet later on, has studied over 3000 married couples and estimates that, for a marriage to survive, there must be a ratio of positive to negative comments of at least 5:1.

It seems fairly obvious to suggest that humans are programmed to focus on failure and disappointment far more than on success and achievement. Usually, it is so automatic that we don't even notice it or the effect that it has on others.

When we are facing change, our brain quickly recalls any previous catastrophes and regenerates those same awful feelings of despair and anxiety. This type of thinking, of course, sends us off on a spiral of negativity, causing us to lose confidence about how well we can cope with change. We are then trapped in a cycle of low confidence, which contributes to a poor performance, which then results in further damage to our self-confidence and even more disappointing results. You're stuck on the hamster wheel of the pessimism cycle.

Dragging their opponents into this pessimism cycle is something that the Australian cricket team has perfected, except they call it 'sledging'. Former captain Mark Waugh speaks with pride about the 'mental disintegration of opponents' before a ball is even bowled by helping them to remember all of their previous failures, weaknesses and mistakes (in pretty graphic detail!). They know that this doesn't help them deliver their best. Yet how often do we face change and start to 'sledge' ourselves?

Stop this happening by making the effort to give at least one unprompted piece of positive feedback a week to the people who you need to engage with your change.

Feeling in control

Tony Blair always wore the same pair of shoes in the House of Commons at Prime Minister's Question Time. During his presidential campaign, Barack Obama played basketball on the morning of every election in his path to the White House. Dr Samuel Johnson always tried to court good fortune by leaving his house right foot first and avoiding treading on cracks in the pavement. President Woodrow Wilson believed the number 13 was lucky for him, as he noted that there were 13 letters in his name and during his thirteenth year at Princeton University he became their thirteenth president. Even Nobel Prize-winning physicist Niels Bohr has a horseshoe over his door. When he was asked if he thought it really brought him good luck, Bohr replied, 'No, but I am told it works whether you believe in it or not.'

Our desire for control is so powerful and the feeling of being in control so rewarding that we often act as though we are controlling the uncontrollable. For instance, people feel more certain that they will win the lottery if they can choose the numbers on the tickets, and feel more confident they will win a dice toss if they can throw the dice themselves.

"We often act as though we are controlling the uncontrollable."

This desire to change and influence things and make things happen is one of the fundamental needs we have. Much of our behaviour from infancy onwards is simply an expression of this penchant for control. Toddlers squeal with delight when they knock over a stack of building blocks, push a ball or squash a cake on their head. Why? Because they did it themselves, that's why.

We come into the world with a passion for control and we leave it in the same way. When we lose our ability to do so, it can cause us to feel stressed, unhappy, hopeless and depressed. And occasionally dead.

In a recent study, researchers gave elderly residents of a nursing home a houseplant. They told half of them that they were in control of the plant's care (this was called the high-control group) and the remaining residents were informed that a member of staff would take responsibility for the plant's wellbeing (this was the low-control group). Just six months later, 30 per cent of the low-control group had died, compared with only 15 per cent of the residents in the high-control group.

To test these findings about the importance of control, a followup study was carried out with the same nursing home residents. Unfortunately, it had an unexpected and tragic ending.

Student volunteers began to pay regular visits to the residents. Those in the high-control group were allowed to control the timing and duration of the visits and the residents in the low-control group were not. After two months, residents in the high-control group reported feeling happier, healthier and more active, and were taking less medication than those in the low-control group.

At this point in the study, the researchers had found what they wanted and so finished their study and stopped the visits. Several months later, a disproportionate number of residents in the high-control group had died. When they had been given control, they had benefited measurably from it but they were inadvertently robbed of control when the study ended.

The virtue of this emotional need for control is also evident within working environments. In one classic study, two groups of people were put into rooms to do puzzles and proofreading while loud, random noises recurred in the background. One group was left alone, while the other was given a button they could press to turn off the sound.

The second group solved five times as many puzzles and made fewer proofreading errors. You can also probably guess that no member of the group ever pressed the button. Knowing it was there and that they controlled it was all that really mattered.

Toyota adopted this principle into its legendary production system, which effectively puts teams of workers in charge of their own production process. Any worker can pull a cord to stop the whole production if they see something that needs to be fixed. The cord is rarely pulled. As with the button, its mere existence – and the control it symbolises – is enough.

Porsche also understands this need for control. At its production plant in Germany, the production line has a subtle difference compared to others in the industry. Instead of an engine rolling along a line of people, each of whom adds a different part, one individual follows the engine from the start of its journey to the end. They have complete control and responsibility for the quality of the engine and, if you know what to look for, on any Porsche engine you will find a mark identifying the technician who made it. The people who make Porsche's engines are very proud of what they do, and Porsche's engines are correspondingly very, very good.

| Change action |

The Churchill test

Winston Churchill recommended that you should make two lists: a list of all the things you can do something about and a list of the things you can't do anything about. He suggested, 'Do something about the things you can do something about – and then go to sleep!'

Take a really close look at the situation that you want to change and figure out exactly what you can and cannot control. It's worth writing these things down. You can then ensure that you focus your energy on the controllables.

It's like going for a job interview. Many people get nervous about the experience and worry about the questions they will be asked and how nice the interviewer will be. When you begin to outline these concerns, it becomes clear that you cannot control what the interviewer will be like or what you'll be asked. There are, however, quite a few things that you can control. Decide on just three. For example:

1. Take a few deep breaths before entering the room to calm down.

2. Slow down and answer questions at a steady pace.

3. Make an effort to enjoy the whole experience.

This is exactly what great athletes do under pressure. They identify a few key controllables and then focus entirely on them. While interviewing rowers at the 1996 Olympics, US sports commentator Charlie Jones spoke to a number of the competing athletes. Any time he asked them a question about something that was outside their control (like the weather, the strengths and weaknesses of their opponents or what might go wrong during a race), the Olympians would respond with the phrase, 'That's outside my boat.'

By refusing to focus on anything beyond their control, these champions were able to bring all their energy to bear on what was within their control. In your own life, focusing exclusively on what's 'in your boat' not only increases your effectiveness, it also reduces your levels of stress dramatically.

You can use a similar approach with others to get them to control the controllables of change – this time by using a traffic light metaphor, which another set of rowing champions, namely Sir Steve Redgrave and his gold medal winning colleagues, used before winning a fifth consecutive Olympic rowing title.

They brainstormed all of the possible distractions that could cost them their victory. They then posted them on a list and ticked them off when they occurred in training, which proved to be an amusing game rather than a distraction.

The group then asked whether these distractions could beat them. They agreed that they couldn't. They then asked what colour would best describe their self-control if they did allow distractions to get the better of them. They answered that they would see red. If they stayed in perfect control and progressed smoothly, then instead they would see green. They also agreed that amber was the moment of decision, when they would choose either to return to green or to go to red. Throughout the Olympic tournament, the team would then have a standard call to 'stay in the green' whenever they felt that a distraction was going to force them to lose focus.

Get your colleagues to detail which things can derail them. Make a list of them and decide how you will deal with them.

Belonging

There is a brilliant scene in Monty Python's *Life of Brian* which highlights the need for belonging. Brian, who is mistaken for the Messiah, speaks to a crowd who are gathered to hear his words. He urges them to think for themselves and tells them, 'Look, you've got it all wrong! You don't need to follow me. You've got to think for yourselves! You're all individuals!' The crowd then chants back in unison, 'Yes! We are all individuals!'

For a long time, it has been commonly agreed that food is the primary motivator behind our need for belonging; in other words, we remain in a group to ensure that we get fed. However, more recent studies on animals have found that this does not necessarily appear to be the case.

A famous example is when animal learning theorists removed baby monkeys from their mother and replaced her with two different substitute mothers: one made from harsh wire and the other made from a soft cloth. Each was fitted with a feeding nipple. Despite our longstanding beliefs, it was found that the infant monkeys became more attached to the substitute soft cloth mother than the harsher wire mother, even when the researchers altered the experiment to ensure that it was only the harsh wire mother who was supplying the food.

These studies are part of a wider body of work on attachment theory. John Bowlby, the psychologist leading the work, believes that we develop attachment between birth and the age of three, based on our experience with caregivers. These are the people we look to for protection, comfort and support. From the way they respond to our needs, we build up a picture of how belonging works and, based on these expectations, from a very early age we develop strategies and ways of ensuring that we belong.

This was further supported by a study conducted by Chicago's School of Nursing, which discovered that 'a lack of a personal sense of belonging' was a greater predictor of depression than any other factors, including poor social support, loneliness and being in conflict with others. The study found that even having strong social support networks, such as having numerous friends or a busy social life, had little impact on how depressed someone was likely to become, unless they felt they really belonged to that particular group.

I regularly adapt my books on change to specific organisations to include the success stories of the staff who work there. Everybody receives a copy of the book. When the books are handed out, the first thing that happens, almost ritualistically, is that everyone rifles through the pages looking for their own name or the names of their friends and colleagues. Many of the employees take the book home to show their family.

Throughout life, the need for attachment continues to be an important part of our identity. Having warm and trusting friendships, feeling that you belong and that others care about you are fundamental to us. Our sense of personal identity and purpose stems largely from our various roles in life and how these roles relate to and depend upon others.

"Throughout life, the need for attachment continues to be an important part of our identity."

Change action

Think of the people who are going to be important in the change you want to create. Write down everyone you can think of and put them into one of three columns:

People I really connect well with	People I think I connect fairly well with	People I don't connect with at all

Look at which column is longest.

- Consider how you treat those people in the first column. How do you behave towards them?
- Looking at those in the second and third columns, what do you think you need to do differently to move them to the left?

▶

This is a technique I use with managers in one retail organi-sation I support. Every month, they will be asked to answer questions about an employee who will have been quizzed earlier in the day. These questions include the names and ages of their children, their last holiday destination and their favourite sports team. Points are awarded for each correct answer. It is a fun and simple way of finding out who they are and are not connecting with.

Safety

Two men are hiking in a forest when they disturb a bear. It is the time of year when bears are easily upset, and true to form the bear comes after them. The men run for their lives. They have a good start on the animal, but four legs are better than two and the bear gets closer and closer. Suddenly one of the men stops, takes off his backpack and sits down on a log.

'What the hell are you doing?' his friend asks, not wanting to stop. He can see the bear's fur boiling as it runs. Its teeth are bared. It's really close.

'I'm changing my shoes,' he replies calmly, removing his heavy hiking boots and slipping on a pair of fancy running shoes.

'You're crazy!' his friend shrieks, running to a spot behind a large tree. 'You'll never outrun a bear, even in those.'

'I don't have to outrun the bear,' the man says, standing up and jogging alongside his friend. 'I only have to outrun you.'

This story illustrates the point that when we think of safety, we presume that it is our personal safety. Although this is true, there is also something to be said for feeling confident to speak up and be yourself without fear of attack.

"There is something to be said for feeling confident to speak up and be yourself without fear of attack."

This was an important point understood by the renowned conductor Benjamin Zander. He works within an industry that has an incredibly high turnover of musicians who play within the rarefied confines of classical orchestras where musicians often suffer from stress and burnout after a short period of time. Although the idea of a concert orchestra being led by a passionate director is a favourite cliché used in lots of leadership training, the irony is that some conductors will be the first to admit they are among the worst examples of dictatorship, with players seething in silent resentment.

'An orchestral player is about the least empowered human being on the planet,' according to Zander, conductor of the Boston Philharmonic. 'In fact, in a study they did at Harvard University of the various professions, they discovered that the orchestral player came in just below prison guards in terms of job satisfaction, which is a tragic observation. The reason is they have no voice and don't feel safe enough to have a say about how they feel.'

Zander had an epiphany about how to change this: 'The conductor of the orchestra is the only musician who doesn't make a sound. The meaning of "symphonia" is "voices sounding together". So the job of the conductor is to make sure every voice is heard. So I did something radical.' He distributed 'this white sheet of paper on the stand of every musician and I encourage them to speak about their feelings without fear'.

Change action

To make change happen, we must have the courage to confront the fears which threaten our safety. By reading this book, you have already shown courage by accepting that change needs to happen. Developing your courage further is much easier if you follow these five key steps:

- Identify which of the specific acts of courage you most need to facilitate change. For example, is it the courage to confront and express yourself or the courage to be confronted and to listen and learn?

- Look at what it costs you to let your anxiety or fear determine your actions instead of making the courageous act. Write out the price you pay, listing examples from your life.

- Create a positive picture of what you want by listing what you gain by accessing and developing that act of courage. Be specific about how you will feel about yourself, how it will improve intimacy or relationship effectiveness, how it will improve your ability to lead, and so forth.

- Select some lower-anxiety opportunities to practise being courageous in real life. Review what and how you did afterwards.

- Congratulate yourself for having had the courage to take action and make the effort. Modify and adjust what you will do next time for even greater effectiveness.

These four big needs are not in any particular order of importance. If any of them are not being addressed, the freeze, flight or fight response is likely to be triggered, increasing the risk of affecting your change effort.

How you perceive the facts of the change you are looking to achieve depends on your attitude towards it. Continue to the next step to find out more.

Step

5

'Attitude is a little thing that makes a big difference.'

Winston Churchill

Understand your reaction to change: interpreting the facts of a situation to determine the outcome

What causes an attitude?

I was once speaking to a conference of leaders and decided that I would start my speech by asking them a question: 'Think of your normal morning routine and tell me, what sort of things happen during that time which can cause you to arrive into work with a *right* attitude?' I emphasised the word 'right'.

Immediately, someone called out 'traffic' and was greeted by a murmur of agreement from the rest of the room. 'The weather' was next, followed by a chorus of other voices offering suggestions such as 'having no milk for your morning cuppa', 'having a row with your partner', 'my boss', 'the job' and 'rude people'. Throughout the exercise, I noticed a man looking increasingly agitated and angry. As the veins in his neck started to bulge, I asked what the cause of his *right* attitude was. Through gritted teeth, he spat out the name of the radio DJ 'Chris Moyles'!

He explained that every morning he would get into his car looking forward to his day's work, but then Chris Moyles would start his show and 'his humour and his choice of music would get on my nerves and put me on edge for the rest of the morning'.

At that very moment, every other person in the room picked their jaws up off the floor and shouted 'Turn it off then!' in unison. It appeared never to have registered with my new friend that he had a number of choices of other stations to listen to on his journey to work.

Now, while this may seem ridiculous, think about the answers you would offer to the same question. How many of your responses would relate to things towards which you have a positive attitude? Or do a lot of them have a negative connotation?

Your response will demonstrate how we all have attitudes to all manner of things. We may call these facts different things, as we have already seen – we may call them people; we may call them the weather, the traffic, situations or circumstances; we may call them the job or where we I live or even our family – but **the reality is that they are all simply facts and our attitude is how we choose to react to them.**

You see, the reality is that there are two types of reaction (which we will call attitude) – positive and negative. Now, in my experience, if three words are ever likely to produce an instant pessimistic response, it's 'positive mental attitude'. I think that the overuse of this concept has left us feeling anaesthetised by these words and the associations they have. Probably because it's been used a lot by senior managers/leaders who want to tell their people to stop moaning and get on with it (whatever it is and however bad it feels to the staff), the concept is often completely misunderstood. It isn't about painting a smile on your face when the entire world is crumbling around you. A person who is positive still recognises that bad things happen – the difference is that they deal with it instead of moaning about it.

"A person who is positive still recognises that bad things happen."

Dislocated expectations

At the Royal Marines training camp in Lympstone, Devon, they recruit their members by putting them through a gruelling selection process, which they claim only the elite will pass.

This involves placing people in a pressurised environment where their reaction to briefs, understanding of briefings, leadership and team-working skills are tested and expanded.

A central part of the assessment is to observe people's reaction to facts when things go wrong. They call this 'Dislocated expectations'. This is because some people think that facts control them, while others think they themselves have far more control. Either way, how people view facts is an external demonstration of their attitude. The criteria can be pared down to a simple question which they ask about each potential Royal Marine: 'Would you go into battle with this person?'

If the answer is yes, it means that you have absolute faith in that potential teammate's attitude to facts and that your life is safe in their hands. The Marines refer to these individuals as 'energisers'. If the answer is no, it is frequently nothing to do with the individual's ability. It is about their attitude and their effect on the team. The Marine's nickname for these people is 'energy sappers'.

There are hundreds of soldiers who can run for three days, think on their feet and handle a weapon. But some of them simply aren't suited to working in a high-pressure team situation. It might be the smallest trait, like a bit of a moan when the going gets tough. Under normal circumstances that wouldn't have any effect. But in high-pressure combat situations just one negative trait can destroy a whole team. The leaders are trained to identify these clues because the consequences are serious. It's the difference between life and death. One wrong team player can drain all the energy from the group.

You see, an attitude is simply a response to facts. It is how we deal with and react to the things that life throws at us on a daily basis.

"An attitude is simply a response to facts."

I would suggest that facts fall into two broad categories. These are:

1. Controllable
2. Uncontrollable.

A few years ago I heard Michael Phelps, the legendary eight-medal Olympic champion swimmer, talk about a simple but very important formula that helped him amass his record medal haul. The formula is:

$$E + R = O$$

(Events + Response = Outcome)

The basic idea is that every outcome you experience in life (whether it is success or failure, wealth or poverty, joy or frustration, or in Phelps's case a gold or silver medal) is the result of how you have responded to the events in your life.

At the age of eight, he first met his coach, Bob Bowman, who asked him, 'Are you going to wait until after you win your first gold medal to have a good attitude? No, you are going to do it beforehand. You have to have the right mental attitude and go from there. You have to be an Olympic champion in attitude long before there's a gold medal around your neck.'

Bowman introduced him to the formula outlined above and suggested that if you don't like the outcomes you are getting, there are two basic choices you can make:

1. **You can blame the event (E) for your lack of results (O).**
   In other words, you can blame the economy, the weather, lack of money, lack of education, gender bias, your partner, the political climate, the system, whatever suits you.

   Bob Bowman would deliberately arrange practices that made Phelps uncomfortable, including altering practice times at late notice, cancelling taxis to take him home and banning him from drinking water in his breaks. He once purposely stepped on Phelps's swimming goggles just moments before a race, forcing him to make do without them.

Phelps could have used these factors ('events') to adopt a negative attitude before he even entered the race. After all, he had plenty of reasons to explain away a defeat. He knew, however, that these were tests to determine how he would respond under pressure.

Remember, his definition of an Olympic attitude is someone who can deal with any event (E) that comes their way. He chose, therefore, to take the second option.

2. **You can instead change your response (R) to the event (E) – the way things are – until you get the outcome you want (O).** You can change your thinking, your language and your behaviour. That is all you really have any control over anyway. Unfortunately, most of us never change our behaviour because we get stuck into conditioned responses.

When Phelps was faced with difficult conditions, he immediately looked at his own reaction and attitude and then asked himself an important question which he dubbed W.I.N.: What's Important Now? Is it complaining or moaning about the hand which fate has dealt you or controlling your reaction?

For example, at the 2008 Olympic Games, Phelps was racing in the final of the 200 metres butterfly, which would bring him the fourth of his eight gold medals. Moments after diving into the pool, Phelps's goggles began to leak, effectively rendering him blind. At this moment, he asked his W.I.N. question and realised that there was no point feeling sorry for himself. Instead, he accepted that he could only control his reaction and adapted his stroke pattern to win the race in a world record time.

By refusing to focus on anything beyond his control, Phelps was able to bring all his energy to bear on what was within his control. In your own life, focusing exclusively on your own W.I.N. question can only improve your effectiveness to create change.

If you look at the things you wrote down before – the things that cause you to have an attitude – then I suspect that the majority of them will fall into the 'uncontrollable' category (E). If that is the case, then think about what you actually *do* have control over. One thing that does fit within your 'controllable' category is your attitude. The attitude that we take to the facts in our lives is a choice. And it is a choice – 100 per cent of the time – irrespective of the fact.

"The attitude that we take to the facts in our lives is a choice."

For example, take the scenario of waking up on Monday morning to the pouring rain. If you look out of the window and let out a moan, that is simply a negative attitude to a fact – a fact over which you have no control and which you cannot change. Or if you get stuck in a traffic jam and it starts to irritate you,

the same applies. Although you cannot control these facts, you can choose how you respond to them. However, as we discussed when understanding our pre-feelings, failing to recognise this can often create a snowball effect, leading to you feeling awful and affecting your behaviour.

President Barack Obama demonstrated this skill during his election campaign. After losing the vote in a key state, he gathered his senior staff and shared with them a handwritten list of observations about the defeat and how they could change their reaction to get a different outcome in future. 'I am not interested in assigning blame. I want to figure out what lessons we can learn and find out how we can do better,' he told his team.

Change action

Take a really close look at whatever it is that you want to change and figure out how the E + R = O formula applies.

For example, you may want to gain support from others for a new idea you want to implement. Now have a look at your behaviour towards achieving this outcome so far.

Event: You need to gain support from your colleagues for a new idea you want to implement.
Response: You became short-tempered and angry with colleagues for their lack of support.
Outcome: You have upset colleagues and have no buy-in to your idea.

Event: You want to lose some weight for your eagerly anticipated summer holiday.
Response: You continue to snack on crisps and chocolate between meals.
Outcome: You are the same weight or heavier but unhappy with your shape.

Event: You want to enjoy getting close to your kids and putting them to bed.

▶

Response: You refuse to say no to your colleagues' requests and end up working late.
Outcome: You arrive home late and too tired to enjoy the experience.

Twelve-step programmes such as Alcoholics Anonymous define insanity as 'continuing the same behaviour and expecting a different result'. If you continue to adopt the same response, your outcome will not change either.

Now apply the Michael Phelps attitude test and look at how you could have changed your response to the facts in order to get a different outcome.

Event: You need to gain support from your colleagues for a new idea you want to implement.
Response: You make time to speak to key people in private and explain your idea in detail.
Outcome: You have improved their understanding and support for the change.

Event: You want to lose some weight for your eagerly anticipated summer holiday.
Response: You prepare healthy snacks to nibble on during the day.
Outcome: You start to lose weight and feel happier with your shape.

Event: You want to enjoy getting close to your kids and putting them to bed.
Response: You meet with your boss and agree a plan to arrive early and leave early on certain days.
Outcome: You arrive home in plenty of time to enjoy the experience.

You've now determined how *you* react to change, but what about the other important people who are supporting your attempts to change? The next step explains how to deal with them.

Step

6

'Me. We.'

...is the shortest poem in the English language. In 1974, after his 'Rumble in the Jungle' fight, Muhammed Ali was invited to address the students of Harvard University. When asked to recite a poem that defined his philosophy of success, he stood up, pointed to himself and said, 'Me.' He then threw his arms wide to the whole audience and said, 'We.'

Anticipate how those around you will react to change: learning to be flexible to get the support you need

Social identity theory: The staffroom test

Imagine going into work on a rainy Monday morning after you have enjoyed a great weekend, which has left you feeling positive and ready to face change head-on. You meet someone who hasn't had the same kind of weekend as you and is not as up for the day. The first words you say are, 'Good morning.' What kind of response do you get? How do some people often respond to those two simple words? Typical examples are, 'Is it?', 'What's good about it?' or just a grunt.

Then you make the fatal mistake and ask the one question you should never ask this type of person on a Monday morning. 'How are you?' How do people respond to that question?

For the next week, actively listen to people's responses. I have collected examples as varied as, 'Not so bad', 'Surviving', 'Can't complain' and 'Fine' to, 'Don't ask', 'What are you on?', 'It's Monday' and 'I'm having a bad year.' My two favourites are, 'As good as they'll let me be' and 'I'm on the crest of a slump.'

In fact, don't just actively listen to these responses. Instead take your own impromptu cultural climate survey. I frequently do this when I go to see a new client.

I recently had reason to visit a struggling business, where I was scheduled to meet the manager. While I was signing the visitors' book, I struck up a conversation with the receptionist. 'Good morning,' I said. 'Morning,' she grunted back. 'How are you?' I offered and received a non-committal shrug in reply. After a few seconds' pause, she enquired about my welfare and asked, 'How are you?' When I thought about her question, I concluded that I felt good and so told her precisely that. My response immediately caused her to start laughing and left me feeling perplexed. What had I said that was so funny? My quizzical expression obviously caused her to explain her unexpected surge of humour. She nodded knowingly and said, in a sinister stage-whisper, 'Wait 'till you get in there. We'll soon knock that out of you!'

Recognising these kinds of comments and the people who make them are important. When Sigmund Freud wrote that 'lieben und arbeit' (love and work) were the keys to happiness, he also said that a key function of work was to connect us to reality and the wider society to which we belong. In other words, work shapes our social identity. What we feel about the identity it gives us is crucially dependent on how others view the organisation or teams we belong to. Psychologists term this the 'social identity theory'.

"Work shapes our social identity."

This theory considers our numerous social identities, which come from our membership of different groups. At any one time, we might belong to a business, a sports team and a group of friends. Once we have established ourselves as belonging to part of that group, we seek to use the membership to enhance our self-esteem.

George Herbert Mead, a social psychologist, observed that our sense of self is to a large extent driven by how others see us, and we start to behave and feel in the way people expect.

This can have an impact on your own reaction to facts – in other words, it shapes your attitude.

I once visited the UK's worst performing school and at the end of the day spent time talking to the newly qualified teachers, who were understandably concerned about starting their careers in such difficult circumstances. I reassured them that the one main difference that would determine whether they would enjoy their teaching careers was not how well they knew their subject, how well they could control a class or even how the school's performance was judged. Instead, it was simply where they chose to sit in the staffroom.

I challenged them to think about whether they wanted to sit with the people who love their job, enjoy the challenge of teaching and love the lifestyle it affords them, or whether they wanted to position themselves next to those who love nothing more than to moan, gripe and bellyache about the job, the management, the canteen and the tea. The attitude of the people they sat with would be contagious.

I had a similar experience when I landed my first ever job, working as a football coach. Before I started, I considered it to be my dream job, playing and coaching football, travelling, being outdoors and having a lot of fun, creativity and freedom. The reality of the job more than lived up to my expectations and I would cycle to work with a beaming grin on my face and count my lucky stars that I had managed to land the best job in the world.

On my first day, I started to form friendships (to belong, in emotional terms). I teamed up with a great set of lads, who kindly showed me the ropes and told me what to do and, just as importantly, what not to do around the place. They warned me who to be careful of upsetting and showed me how to navigate my way around the less than inspiring parts of the job. In other words, they explained the unwritten ground rules of the company culture.

It was only after I had been there for a couple of months when I was asked by my mum how work was. I offered a non-committal shrug and a grunt of 'All right'. She asked what the problem was. I was bemused; there wasn't a problem. The job was the same as I had been doing since day one. 'So why has it gone from being "the best job in the world",' my mum asked, 'to now being just "all right"?' The answer was obvious. The social identity theory had taken effect. It was where I had chosen to sit in the staffroom.

The group I had chosen to belong to had a more cynical attitude to the realities of the job than I did. Expressing enthusiasm wasn't the done thing and, although I wasn't aware of it, during my first few months I had subconsciously adopted this same attitude in my attempts to fit in and belong.

We've established that you need to have a positive attitude to improve your chances of success in creating change; however, it's equally vital that you take the time to identify whether those people who you surround yourself with are hindering or assisting your positive attitude. Equally, if you are trying to change through others you need to understand how you can influence their attitude too. Let's have a look at some tips to do just that.

"Identify whether those people who you surround yourself with are hindering or assisting your positive attitude."

Crab mentality

As we have seen, when looking at our emotional needs a sense of belonging is key. The sociologist Dr Wayne Dyer agrees and suggests that **every one of us needs to belong to a tribe or group, which operates to its own certain guidelines. Fitting in with these is vital as many of them ensure the tribe's survival, but many of them can also hold the gifted individual back.** Here is how Dr Dyer describes it: 'Let go of the idea that the tribe is going to give approval. When you are learning anything that is outside the parameters of the tribe, what you are doing is saying, "I am going to evolve at a faster rate." But if you go to the tribe and tell them that, immediately you're going to be put in your place.'

Dyer's observation often reminds me of a quote from Rudyard Kipling's second *Jungle Book*:

'Now this is the Law of the Jungle

As old and as true of the sky

And the wolf that keeps it may prosper

And the wolf that shall break it must die.

As the creeper that circles the tree trunk

The Law runneth forward and back

The strength of the pack is the wolf

And the strength of the wolf is the pack.'

Continuing with the animal theme, if you've ever seen a bucket of crabs, you will be familiar with the following behaviour. When one crab tries to crawl out of the bucket, the others pull him back in, to be later boiled and eaten along with everybody else. If it wasn't for the other crabs pulling each other back into the bucket, they could each get out on their own!

Researchers Pat Heim and Susan Murphy have studied organisations and drawn similar conclusions. They call it the 'power-dead-even rule', which lies at the heart of office politics. We all have an idea of where we fit in a social structure. Our status and that of everyone else is in balance. If something changes that – someone is promoted, rewarded or favoured in some way – then people take action to redress the balance, which can include all the typical tricks of office – and playground – politics.

Before we move on to think about those people you spend most of your time with, let's look at the four different types you may encounter.

My kind of people?

The psychologist David Kantor once led what many people have suggested was the first incarnation of reality TV. In an effort to study how schizophrenia manifests in family systems, Kantor set up cameras in various rooms of people's houses, then pored over hours of footage of these people's lives. Kantor soon detected a pattern that emerged again and again within every group dynamic, regardless of whether schizophrenia was a factor.

In analysing tapes of the families he studied, Kantor found that every family had members who fell into four distinct roles.

The first role was that of the initiator: the person who always has ideas, likes to start projects and advocates new ways of moving forward. Those in the second group are the initiators' opposites – blockers. Whatever new idea the initiator comes up with, the blocker finds fault with it. 'Let's go to Disneyland!' says the initiator. 'No. It's too expensive,' retorts the blocker. 'Let's start a new company.' 'Most fail within the first year.'

If hanging out with initiators makes us want to go out and do something fun, spending a minute with blockers makes us reluctant to do anything. Of course, it is easy to think of blockers as pure curmudgeons, but we will see that they do play a vital role in maintaining balance within a group.

Initiators and blockers are bound to lock horns, which is where those in the third group – supporters – step in, taking one side or the other. If there is a decision to be made, you can bet on the supporter siding with either the initiator or the blocker. The fourth role is that of the detached observer, who stays disengaged and neutral, tending merely to comment on what is going on.

It is possible that people can change roles according to what the specific issue is. For example, if I think buying a new car is a good idea I'd be an initiator, but if I don't then I might be a blocker. If I don't really care about the issue I might simply be an observer.

Although there is never a definitive conclusion for these four personality types, an understanding can be good enough. If you want to do a little extra research, the good news is that it could be enjoyable. All you need to do is to put on a DVD of the *Star Wars* films. Four of the major characters neatly represent the four different types of attitude. Let's look at each in turn.

Type 1: Han Solo, the initiator

Han Solo is a hot-headed, risk taking, freelance smuggler, also an ace pilot, a master blaster and a high-stakes gambler. In many ways, Han Solo is adventurous and easily bored; he is constantly pushing on and through. He speaks like a true initiator when he is being chased by enemy ships and says, 'We'll be safe enough once we make the jump to hyperspace. Besides, I know a few manoeuvres. We'll lose them. Here's where the real fun begins.'

Although he initially claims that money is his true motivator, he soon demonstrates that he really wants to be respected. When he tells Luke Skywalker, 'Never tell me the odds,' this is because, like all initiators, he is motivated by challenge, excitement and by getting things done. They want to get to the point fast and, ideally, first. And then on to the next thing, and then the next. They like to have demanding goals with clear outcomes and preferably a complimentary element.

If a situation doesn't have a clear direction, an initiator can become frustrated. Han Solo dismisses thoughts about the power of the Jedi Knights by telling them, 'I've seen a lot of strange stuff, but I've never seen anything to make me believe there's one all-powerful force controlling everything. There's no mystical energy field that controls my destiny.'

"If a situation doesn't have a clear direction, an initiator can become frustrated."

If initiators are given a suitable challenge to create change and then left to their own devices, they will make things happen and quickly. Han solo boasts to Princess Leia, 'You know, sometimes, I amaze even myself.' They consider it generally better to make a decision, even if it turns out to be the wrong one, than put things off. They are more likely to initiate something than complete it – they like to get the ball rolling but will avoid organising and implementing if they can.

Type 2: C-3PO, the blocker

C-3PO is a fussy but loyal, hard-working protocol droid, who offers a touch of comic relief in *Star Wars* with his constant worries about the dangers and discomforts he faces. He is rebuffed when he attempts to remind Luke Skywalker, 'The chances of survival are seven hundred and seventy-five...to one.'

C-3PO believes that attention to detail is everything. Whereas initiators are keen to move on to the next challenge, C-3PO would rather finish the one he is doing properly. When he is mistaken for a god by the Ewoks, he refuses to comply and argues, 'It's against my programming to impersonate a deity.'

Blockers are often motivated by doing something very well, including delivering the Death Star plans to the Rebels – they want the best possible solution, and once they commit they will be inclined to do whatever it takes to get it.

The blocker's mantra is the saying, 'If a job's worth doing, it's worth doing well.' The blocker's desire for things to be right means that they are often the first to spot gaps or errors and to challenge assumptions about the way things are done. They value being given the freedom and independence to think things through by themselves. Their desire for self-sufficiency means that they can be hard to get to know.

Type 3: Yoda, the observer

In *Star Wars*, Yoda, the 900-year-old revered Jedi Master, is the character who wants harmony within the galaxy. He has every confidence that, in the long run, personal freedom will win out over the tyranny of the Dark Side: 'The more they tighten their grip, the more star systems will slip through their fingers.'

An observer merely sits back and watches the action take place, choosing to comment on facts rather than offer opinions. When the wise old Jedi Master listened to Luke Skywalker express doubts about his ability to beat Darth Vader and conquer the Dark Side, he offered the comment, 'Either do or do not. There is no try.'

Type 4: Luke Skywalker, the adapter

Luke is the character at the heart of the group. Without Luke, Han Solo, C-3PO and Yoda might seem a little disparate. With Luke, who is in many ways a bit like all of them, it all makes sense.

As his name suggests, he is a romantic dreamer and heir to the mystical Jedi Knights, the benevolent champions of the Republic and ministers of the Force – the spiritual life energy that binds the galaxy together. Once he decides to learn 'the ways of the Force and become a Jedi like my father', he begins a journey to find the wisdom and power of human intuition, learning to 'let go of my conscious self', to 'stretch out with my feelings' and to 'trust my feelings'.

Adapters are people who are a combination of the other three styles. They see the merits in focusing on people, getting things done and quality of performance. They value flexibility and taking a balanced approach to any situation.

They can often take on the role of peacekeeper in a disagreement as they can quickly see and empathise with each of the different perspectives. It is Luke who tries to convince others that Darth Vader is still capable of changing, claiming, 'There is still good in him.'

Adapters like to experiment, be open to change, make sure bases are covered and options considered. They sometimes feel pulled in many directions by their different motivations. Luke goes through the wringer when Darth Vader urges him to 'Give yourself to the Dark Side. It is the only way you can save your friends.'

So, which character do you most identify with? Are you a blocker, initiator, observer or adapter?

Our innate sense of belonging means that we often seek out similar types of people. For example, initiators often seek out other initiators, people who will encourage their thinking about what is possible. In Napoleon Hill's classic book *Think and Grow Rich*, he dedicates a whole chapter to the benefits – financial and emotional – of this. Hill writes: 'No two minds ever come together without, thereby, creating a third, invisible, intangible force which may be likened to a third mind.'

Famous examples of this include US President Benjamin Franklin who created the Leather Apron Club, a group of young men who met weekly to discuss subjects such as philosophy, morals, economics and politics. The group existed for 40 years and eventually became the American Philosophical Society, the works of which are still evident today. The group was responsible for the implementation of the first public library, volunteer fire departments, the first public hospital, police departments and even paved streets. They adhered to Napoleon Hill's belief, 'When a group of individual brains are co-ordinated and function in harmony, the increased energy created through that alliance becomes available to every individual brain in the group.'

It is easy to see why people are naturally attracted to initiators. They bring energy and a buzz. In the 1980s Toyota received half a million ideas from its staff about how to do things better. This was an average of 12 ideas per employee per year. Management encouraged these initiators to speak up and contribute and implemented 85–90 per cent of the ideas put forward. It is partly this initiative that is credited with helping Toyota to enjoy its status as the world's second largest car manufacturer today.

Most of the tension in any group lies between the initiator and the blocker. Initiators are all about making things happen. They have a wealth of fresh ideas. They might be wildly optimistic and have a tendency to rush into action, and their creativity, energy and drive can be instrumental when it comes to innovation. In contrast, blockers question the merit or wisdom of new decisions. Instead of going along with things, they raise points about what they see are the harmful consequences that might follow.

"Most of the tension in any group lies between the initiator and the blocker."

It is dangerous simply to dismiss the importance of this latter group. Blockers can be useful. When the space programme came to a successful conclusion with the 1969 moon landing, the chief scientist pointedly thanked all of the blockers who had told him that it would never happen – particularly those who gave him a long list of reasons why not. He believed that these people had done the designing for him, because a careful assessment of those lists gave him a blueprint, including the need to create a whole new branch of chemistry (boron chemistry) to deliver the programme.

Similarly, think how American politicians and the media reacted to the French during the days leading up to the second Iraq war. At the time, taking on the role of the initiator, the US administration gave countless arguments to convince politicians and other nations to join America in war. The White House officials motivated, energised and pushed forward, and before long managed to get public opinion on their side.

When George Bush tried to get a UN resolution passed in support of the war in Iraq, the French foreign minister tried to block the measure, firmly announcing, 'We will not allow a resolution to pass that authorises resorting to force.' President Jacques Chirac requested that UN inspectors be allowed to get on with looking for weapons of mass destruction without US intervention and they were quickly branded as blockers and obstructionists. Congress got so upset that it passed a resolution officially renaming the Capitol cafeteria's French fries 'freedom fries'. In true blocker fashion, the French embassy retorted, 'We are dealing with very serious issues and not the name given to potatoes.'

In retrospect, the French argument should have merited more careful attention. But because they so conveniently fitted the role of the blocker, they were seen as a thorn in Bush's side.

As tempting as it is to dismiss them, blockers do play a vital role in maintaining balance in a group. A blocker can function as the brakes to prevent a trip down a potentially disastrous route. Even if a blocker's opinion is wrong, at least it adds a perspective to the debate and gives others an opportunity to look at things in a different light. The famous explorer Ernest Shackleton dealt with the blockers in his exploration groups by assigning them to sleep in his own tent. When he separated them to work in groups on chores, he grouped the blockers with him. This way, he was able to minimise their negative influence while allowing him to listen to their feedback.

"Blockers do play a vital role in maintaining balance in a group."

Political scientists have shown in a series of studies of juries that, when someone is prepared to represent the minority viewpoint, it makes a group more balanced and its decision-making process more rigorous. This is true even when the minority viewpoint turns out to be ill-conceived. The confrontation with a dissenting view forces people to look at their own positions more seriously. This doesn't mean that the ideal jury will follow the plot of *Twelve Angry Men*, where a single hold-out convinces 11 men who are ready to convict that they're all wrong. But it does mean that having even a single different opinion can make a group wiser.

Change action

1. Make a list of up to 15 people who are essential to your change challenge.

2. Now put the names of these people in the relevant box in the grid below in terms of how helpful and supportive they are.

   Tip: There are no right or wrong answers here and it doesn't mean that a person is good or bad. It is about how supportive they are of you in terms of your change challenge. Remember, a person can also change their role depending on the specific issue.

3. Look at your list and decide if the balance is helpful. Is there any action you want to take to move someone from one box to another? For example, ask an adapter for help and support to become an initiator. You can do this in a number of simple ways:

   - Give the four types a character from a popular film or show (the writers of *Sex and the City* actually based their four main characters on this model). You can ask people to pretend to be that character for a certain meeting. When they try it, you can ask them to think about the strengths and weaknesses of that type without causing offence to people believing you are attacking their own personal character.

- Before starting your change challenge, outline the details to others and get them to identify which box they fit in with regard to the specific task. This is an incredibly helpful way of initiating the discussion of where you need people to be and why.
- Throughout the task, check what people are feeling and how they are responding. This allows you to keep focused on areas that need to be addressed quickly.

Initiator – *really active; supportive and helpful; encouraging; interested*	Blocker – *highlights the problems/difficulties*
Adapter – *don't really understand; not aware*	Observer – *not bothered in the slightest*

I'd now like you to pause for a second. I suspect that if you reflect on what you have read, you will know that what we have discussed so far is common sense.

As I mentioned at the start of Step 5, the difficulty that many people have with this material is with the idea of group hugging, high-fiveing, massaging the shoulders of the person standing next to you or looking in the mirror in the morning, smiling at the reflection and instructing yourself to 'be positive'. These just don't sit well with most of us. Attitude isn't about this, it is how we respond to the facts of a situation. The way we interpret facts is largely down to our beliefs, and that's the next stop on our change mission.

Step

7

'One person with a belief is a social power equal to ninety-nine who have only interests.'

John Stuart Mill, economist

Examine your beliefs: using your beliefs to promote change

In order to build interest in his travelling show, the great escape artist Harry Houdini would frequently arrive in a town early and challenge the local jailer to try to keep him locked in a cell. If he couldn't escape within an hour, he would offer the jailer a $1000 reward.

In one town, he made the challenge and was dutifully ushered into a jail cell. As soon as the door clanged shut behind him, he began trying to find a way out. As the minutes slipped by, he soon found that this escape was going to be tougher than

he had expected. He tried every trick, but he couldn't find a way out. At the end of the time, the jailers found him sitting in the middle of the cell sobbing in frustration. He had failed.

The biggest surprise came when the jailer discovered that he had forgotten to lock the door. Houdini could have walked out any time he wanted just by pushing the door open. The irony was that this escape route was one that he had never considered. An unlocked door!

This story is a great example of how our own beliefs can sometimes act as locked doors in our minds. But where do they come from?

"Our own beliefs can sometimes act as locked doors in our minds."

Natural born beliefs

Did you pop out of the womb with all of your current beliefs already hard-wired in? Think about it.

The answer is no. Psychologists tell us that we are born with only two fears (which are the nearest equivalent to beliefs). One is a fear of falling and the other is a fear of loud noises, and both are related to the birth experience. These are the only beliefs that you have in the first few seconds after you arrive on the earth. You acquire everything else. This is something that we will explore in more detail later.

We all have deep-rooted beliefs which will either limit or inspire us, but all too often we seem to build more of the former than the latter. In the movie *Chicken Run*, the chickens who are trying to break out of their chicken-wire world to escape their fate at the chopping block are led by a feisty little hen named Ginger, who reminds them, 'The fences are all in your mind.' The biggest obstacle other than the physical fences they're surrounded by are the mental fences that hold them captive. When we build from the perspective of limiting beliefs, beliefs that say, 'I just can't', 'I'll never be able to do that', 'It's just not who I am', we also build fences in our mind that are so high we can't ever get past them.

Bringing about change often requires self-belief. So how can we overcome those beliefs that are holding us back?

Beliefs = Perceptions

Our beliefs are formed by the way we perceive and interpret the world. Read the sentence below, just once. Once you have done this, count the number of times you see the letter F in that sentence.

FINISHED FILES ARE THE RESULT OF MANY YEARS
OF SCIENTIFIC STUDY COMBINED WITH
THE EXPERIENCE OF MANY YEARS.

How many Fs are there? The vast majority of us will see two or three. Some of you may see four or five. Some of you may have recognised that the correct answer is six. The chances are that if you didn't spot this number, it was because you missed the ones hidden within the word 'of'.

Why is this the case? When you read the sentence through you may have looked at the word 'of' and read it phonetically as 'ov'. It tells you that you can't possibly have the letter F in it because you have read it through and stored it as a V. In other words, your perception created a belief in the number of Fs there are.

Take a moment to think about yourself. What beliefs do you have about your ability to create the change you want? Beliefs are mightily powerful tools which impact on your performance, good or bad.

"What beliefs do you have about your ability to create the change you want?"

Quite often, we will base our answer on our first or past experience of creating change. I wonder how many times you have come across that. How often do people base their ability (or lack of it) upon their past ability (or inability)?

Dr Leonard Orr suggests that within every one of us there are two people – one is a thinker, the other is a prover. The thinker, who corresponds to your conscious mind, is the part of you that thinks up ideas and generates possibilities. The prover, who approximates to your unconscious mind, has the job of collecting just the right facts to support whatever it is that the thinker thinks. Orr's law, as described by author Robert Anton Wilson, is 'Whatever the thinker thinks, the prover proves.'

This may sound too far-fetched but I see it all the time in organisations facing change. When an organisation asks me to work with its people to help make change happen or implement a new project, watching people react to change is fascinating. Perhaps they have experienced a similar change before in a different organisation where it failed. In cases like this, the belief of those people – that it didn't work then and won't work now – gets transmitted to others who have no experience of the change. Ultimately, what happens? Does the change succeed or fail?

This same kind of phenomenon can also occur when we attach a label to ourselves or others. This is merely a label of our beliefs which can become self-perpetuating. In psychological circles, this is known as the Pygmalion effect (describing how we take on the positive traits assigned to us) and the Golem effect (describing how we take on the negative traits).

In the late 1960s, the psychologists Robert Rosenthal and Lenore Jacobsen conducted an experiment to look at the impact of beliefs on educational achievements. They randomly selected a group of children and told teachers that some of them could be expected to be 'late bloomers' because of their results in what was a non-existent test of ability. The children identified were, in fact, no different from the other children.

Rosenthal and Jacobsen then sat back and waited to see what impact, if any, changing the teachers' beliefs might have on the children's subsequent achievement. They reported their findings in the seminal book *Pygmalion in the Classroom*. Slowly but surely, those children labelled as having great potential started to pull ahead. The fact that the teachers had greater expectations of them and gave them the opportunity to excel simply helped to make their beliefs a self-fulfilling reality.

Since then, there have been over 400 studies on self-fulfilling expectancy effects. A great example of this was a study conducted within the Israeli army, when 105 soldiers were about to participate in a gruelling 15-week commander training process.

Before the training sessions started, psychologists informed the training officers leading the programme that the army had already accumulated comprehensive data on each of the trainees, including psychological test scores, data from previous courses and ratings by previous commanders.

Based on this information, the officers were told that each soldier had been classified into one of three 'command potential' (CP) categories: high, regular and unknown (due to insufficient information). The trainees had no idea that this was going on and the trainers weren't aware that the 'command potential' scores were completely bogus and had been randomly assigned to the soldiers with no relevance to their actual ability.

At the end of the course, 15 weeks later, they discovered something remarkable. When the soldiers completed a test to assess how much they had learned over the course, the soldiers who had been labelled as having high potential performed much better (79.9 per cent average) than their unknown and regular counterparts (who scored 72 per cent and 65 per cent respectively). Simply being labelled, however arbitrarily, as having a high leadership potential translated into actual improved ability.

Another study by psychologists suggested that these same effects operate in the workplace, schools and our home lives. If you have ever been fortunate enough to work for a boss who values and believes in your ability, you will know that you tend to rise to meet their high expectations. This is why many organisations have high potential schemes for those employees they believe have the potential to go far. On the other hand, what is the impact on other employees who don't receive this same recognition? I once worked in an organisation which labelled some of its staff as 'non-critical' and 'semi-skilled'. They frequently wondered why these employees were some of the poorest performers.

The crucial point to understand here is that people behave not according to reality, but rather based on their perception of reality. Or, to put it another way, their belief about what is real. We all have limits, but so many of these limits have nothing to do with our genetic makeup. Many of our limits – the things that we believe we can or can't do – are self-imposed or imposed on us by others.

"Many of our limits are self-imposed or imposed on us by others."

When creating change, your beliefs about who you are – what you believe you can or can't do – ultimately play a significant part in how effective you will be, so it's now important to check whether these beliefs fall into the most common traps that can derail our change effort.

Step

8

'Obstacles are those frightful things we see when we take our eyes off the goal.'

Henry Ford

Avoid belief traps: spotting the most common mistakes that hinder change

Belief traps

There are three typical mistakes to be aware of when analysing your beliefs about change.

1. Results-based beliefs

I often hear people claim, 'The reason I have great self-belief is because I am really good at...'

What's wrong with that? This is nothing other than results-based thinking. The challenge with this is that we might have to wait a long time to get the results we are waiting for. It would be awful if we could only have self-belief and a positive attitude when things are going well for us. The time we need self-belief most is when things are not going well. Anyone can be positive in good times.

"The time we need self-belief most is when things are not going well."

If you think about it, every time someone achieves something for the first time, by definition, the belief has to precede the result. It cannot be any other way and yet too often we slip into the results-based approach. How often do you hear a sportsperson being interviewed and say, 'I need one good win and everything will be all right'?

I once ran a session with a rugby team during a period of poor results. We spoke about the impact of their beliefs. One of the senior members of the team asked me if I was suggesting that if they believed 100 per cent that they would win the league, that I would 100 per cent guarantee that it would happen.

My answer was a simple no. It doesn't work like that. But I did give him two guarantees:

1. A 100 per cent negative limiting belief pretty much guarantees a 100 per cent negative result. I can't think of a situation where from a starting point of a 100 per cent negative belief I have ever achieved anything other than a negative result.

2. A 100 per cent positive and inspirational belief gives me a 100 per cent best chance of achieving the result I want.

Sir Alex Ferguson outlined this philosophy in his own unique way. When he was asked about Manchester United's success, he claimed that it was based on the belief that 'Manchester United never get beaten. We may occasionally run out of time but we never believe we can be beaten.'

However, none of us is born with any beliefs. If that is the case, who or what gives us and helps us to formulate these beliefs? The answer relates back to the point in the 'attitude' chapter (Step 5) and the people with whom we surround ourselves.

Ben Carson is a great example of this. He had a tough childhood in America. His father left home, his mother was in and out of work and he and his brother were always in trouble at school. Because they were a 'welfare family', they were constantly moving from one town to another in search of work.

Ben's schoolwork was poor and he decided that if he was going to be thrown out of school, he didn't want to be labelled as 'stupid'. When he did so badly in maths that he became embarrassed, he threw over a desk and got thrown out of class for being 'aggressive' instead. This became a habit. Whenever a class got hard, he would go crazy and get thrown out again.

Eventually, his mother got sick of this and told him and his brother that she would mark their homework every night. She marked everything and would praise them for their good work.

Ben started to do better at school and showed that he was actually pretty bright. One day he asked his mother to help him with some schoolwork. 'Ben,' she told him, 'I can't read.' He was amazed. All that time, his mother had been setting him work, marking it and praising him for how clever he was, when the reality was that she couldn't tell how good or bad his work actually was.

The important thing is that Ben's mother helped him to start thinking and then believing that he was quite smart. Once he started to believe it, he started to perform well after years of failure and misery.

By the way, that little boy, Ben Carson, now works at John Hopkins Hospital in Baltimore, Maryland, and grew up to be one of the world's leading paediatric neurosurgeons. He works with children who suffer from a rare form of epilepsy and pioneered a surgical procedure called hemispherectomy, and found that children who had the operation not only made a full recovery but started to pick up things that they had lost the ability to do before the operation.

2. Ludic fallacy

Another mistake which is commonly made about change-creating beliefs is when we become trapped by the ludic fallacy. Nassim Nicholas Taleb coined this phrase in his book *The Black Swan*. It is when you believe in only the things that you know are possible.

Think of the great discoveries of our time – Columbus setting sail to the edge of a world considered to be flat; Edison discovering light without heat; Wilbur and Orville Wright achieving the very first powered flight; Neil Armstrong setting foot on the moon. These were all achieved by people who refused to let their own horizons represent the limits of what can be achieved. Look at your own change challenges in a naïve manner and follow the advice of George Bernard Shaw, who said, 'I dream things that never were and I say, "Why not?"' and then see how much you can really achieve.

"Look at your own change challenges in a naïve manner and see how much you can really achieve."

It was a failure to observe the ludic fallacy that once rocked the Las Vegas casino industry to its core.

When doing the risk planning to ensure that the casinos could guard against losing money, the bosses looked at a range of possible scenarios. These included creating a mind-boggling series of defence systems to stop gamblers working out how to cheat the casino. Despite this, they still lost over $100 million due to the completely unexpected situation of a white Bengal tiger losing its temper.

One of the major Las Vegas attractions was the Siegfried and Roy show, a long-running illusion and magic act. Siegfried and Roy used white lions and tigers as part of the act. They reared the animals themselves and allowed them to sleep in their bedrooms. Nobody ever believed that these powerful animals would ever turn against their masters – except in October 2003, when Montecore the tiger suddenly bit into Roy's neck during a live show, causing him serious injuries. The show was cancelled, business was lost and bad publicity damaged the casino's reputation, all because the bosses had made the mistake of believing only in what they knew was possible.

This story always reminds me of the wonderful conversation between Alice and the Queen in Lewis Carroll's *Alice in Wonderland*:

"'There's no use trying," said Alice, "one can't believe in impossible things."

"I daresay you haven't had much practice," said the Queen.

"When I was your age I always did it for half an hour a day.

Why, sometimes I've believed as many as six impossible things before breakfast."'

My favourite story about overcoming the ludic fallacy relates to a Ford motorcar dealer. In the early days of the company, when all Ford sold were open-topped Model Ts, all dealers throughout America closed during the winter as it was thought it wouldn't be possible to sell open-topped cars at this inclement time of year. During the winter break, Henry Ford himself decided to do a tour of his most successful dealers to see how he could help them when they reopened in the summer. Arriving during a heavy snowstorm at his most successful dealership – a place that sold nearly twice as many cars as everyone else – Ford was surprised to see it open. He summoned the manager and asked him what he thought he was doing selling cars in the middle of winter. The manager replied, 'Sorry Mr Ford, nobody ever told us we had to close.'

3. Learned helplessness

Of all the beliefs about change, the most dangerous trap is taking instances of failure and generalising them. This phenomenon in psychology is known as learned helplessness – the self-fulfilling belief that nothing we do will make any difference.

It was this tactic that was adopted with devastating consequences in the Korean war. Major Doctor William E. Mayer, who would later become the US Army's chief psychiatrist, studied a thousand American prisoners of war who had been detained in a North Korean camp, as he was particularly interested in examining one of the most extreme and effective cases of psychological warfare on record.

American soldiers had been detained in camps that were not considered especially cruel or unusual by conventional standards. The captive soldiers had adequate food, water and shelter. They weren't subjected to common physical torture tactics such as having bamboo shoots driven under their fingernails. In fact, fewer cases of physical abuse were reported in North Korean POW camps than in prison camps from any other major military conflict in history.

Why then did so many American soldiers die in these camps? They weren't hemmed in with barbed wire. Armed guards didn't surround the camps. Yet no soldier ever tried to escape. Furthermore, these men regularly broke rank and turned against each other, sometimes forming close relationships and bonds with their captors. Even after they were released to a Red Cross group in Japan, they were given the chance to phone loved ones to let them know they were alive. Very few bothered to make the call. When they did eventually return home, the soldiers maintained no friendships or relationships with each other. Mayer described each man as mentally being in a 'solitary confinement cell without any steel or concrete'.

How could this have happened? The answers were found in the extreme mental tactics that the North Korean captors used. They employed what Mayer described as the 'ultimate weapon' of war. Through his research in these camps, Mayer had discovered an extreme case of learned helplessness. The soldiers actually called this 'give-up-itis' although the official medical term offered was *mirasmus*, meaning, in Mayer's words, 'a lack of resistance, a passivity, a learned helplessness'.

Despite relatively minimal physical torture, *mirasmus* raised the overall death rate in the North Korean POW camps to an incredible 38 per cent – the highest POW death rate in US military history. Even more astounding was that half of these soldiers died because they had given up. They had completely surrendered, both mentally and physically.

The captors gathered groups of ten to twelve soldiers and employed what Mayer described as 'a corruption of group psychotherapy'. In these sessions, each man was required to stand up in front of the group and confess all the bad things he had done – as well as all the good things he could have done but had failed to do so.

The most important part of this tactic was that the soldiers were not 'confessing' to the North Koreans, but to their own peers. By subtly eroding the care, trust, respect and social acceptance among their fellow American soldiers, the North Koreans created an environment in which goodwill was constantly and ruthlessly drained.

In one case, 40 men stood by as three of their extremely ill fellow soldiers were thrown out of their mud hut by a comrade and left to die in the elements. Why did they do nothing to help their fellow soldiers? Because it 'wasn't their job'. The relationships had been broken; the soldiers simply didn't care about each other any more.

Beliefs = Behaviour = Results

I am not saying it is easy to change your beliefs, but **what you believe, usually at a deep, subconscious level, will determine how you behave on a consistent basis, and this will determine how successful you are in making change happen.** Put simply, if you change the beliefs then you will change the results. Let's try it with your change challenge.

"If you change the beliefs then you will change the results."

In the dock

This is a process that helps you to test your beliefs about whatever it is you want to change. Many schools of personal development use techniques based on these principles to uncover what tricks your belief system may be playing on you. I love this technique because of its power in helping us to determine where to focus our energy in order to bring about change.

In today's society we often find that our minds work at 100 mph – like toddlers who have had too many sugary drinks and just can't keep still. Within all this chaos our minds are telling us things; this is our internal dialogue or voices in our heads.

It is time to listen to these voices and put them in the dock. To flush these out we need the help of our angels and devils, the ones who sit on either shoulder and whisper.

- **Devil.** Think of something you want to change and allow yourself to be negative and devilish. Next, with no censoring, write your beliefs down about the issue you want to change or challenge from a weasely negative point of view. It's fun to be wicked and so don't analyse or restrict yourself, just scribble wildly.

- **Angel.** Now, to balance things up a bit, do it from your angel's perspective. Be loving and nurturing, see the good and be optimistic. It might feel odd but go for it anyway.

By now you should have two lots of outpourings that contain your beliefs about the change challenge you face. It is now time to put them in the dock.

Action

First, get into a positive state. Shake off the angels and demons. Picture yourself feeling strong and confident. Read through each statement and ask, 'Is that true, false or don't know?'

True is something that is provable. It should stand up in a court of law. There is no judgement involved. False is the stuff you know deep down is rubbish. Watch out here because your brain is tricky and will often phrase things in a nebulous and airy-fairy way that sounds true. Be strict – if it is not absolutely true, it can only be false or don't know.

Sometimes you will find statements that could be true but you are not absolutely certain. If it is a prediction – for instance, 'I will be less successful' – it can be at best a don't know because you cannot predict the future. However, 'Everyone will hate me' is false because there is no way that it can be true. If in doubt, write the statement again using language that is definitely true.

Example: *Getting fit*

Devil	True/False/ Don't know	Angel	True/False/ Don't know
I can't be bothered to stick at it.	FALSE	It's good for you.	TRUE
It won't last long anyway.	DON'T KNOW	When I'm fit, I feel better about myself.	TRUE
It's hard work.	DON'T KNOW	I love some sports.	TRUE
It's no fun.	FALSE	I can do a little every day.	TRUE
I'll only be disappointed.	DON'T KNOW	Exercising gives me more energy.	TRUE
It's a waste of time.	FALSE	I want to be fitter.	TRUE
I won't notice the difference.	FALSE	I'll look great in my tight shirts.	DON'T KNOW
It takes lots of time.	FALSE	I feel good in my tight shirts when I feel fitter.	TRUE
I don't want it to be a fad.	TRUE		
It takes effort.	TRUE		

Example: *Worrying about giving a presentation*

Devil	True/False/ Don't know	Angel	True/False/ Don't know
I haven't prepared enough.	FALSE	I know this stuff better than anyone.	TRUE
I'm out of my depth.	FALSE	This is a great opportunity for me to show what I can do.	TRUE
I'll really cock this up.	FALSE	They want me to do well.	TRUE
They will catch me out and make me look stupid.	FALSE	I'll have all their attention.	TRUE
I'll go blank and forget everything I've prepared.	DON'T KNOW	If I set it up my way, the whole session will be fun.	TRUE
They want it to go wrong.	FALSE	I can do it my way.	TRUE
They'd love me to look stupid.	FALSE	I can give them a great experience compared to the rest of their day.	TRUE
I'll never live this down.	FALSE	I can learn from it and get better each time.	TRUE
My career here is over.	FALSE	I can wear my new, sexy suit!	TRUE
		It gives me a chance to hang out with the bosses.	TRUE
		I can use this chance to get their input and make it better.	TRUE

You now have a greater understanding of your beliefs about change. But where do these beliefs come from? Read on to discover.

Step

9

Reporter interviewing a 104-year-old woman:

"What's the best thing about being 104?"

"That's easy. No peer pressure."

Be aware of where you're sitting: understanding what influences you to find the key to change

We are all familiar with the famous words of Neil Armstrong, the first man on the moon: 'One small step for a man. One giant leap for mankind.' What's less well known is that he added a phrase under his voice: 'Over to you, Mr Blatsky.'

When asked about this he would say it was a private joke. But during a lecture tour of American colleges in 1995 he was quizzed about it again. After a pause he replied that he could now explain it, as sadly Mr Blatsky had passed on. His answer was a tribute to the power of conditioning.

Armstrong explained how he had grown up living next door to the Blatskys. One day he heard an argument between them. Mrs Blatsky was shouting, 'Sex?! You want oral sex? You'll get oral sex when...when that kid next door walks on the moon!' Over to you, Mr Blatsky...

In the last chapter we saw that our beliefs can change the way we appreciate experiences. The main factor that creates these beliefs is our conditioning. Like Pavlov's famous dogs (that learned to salivate at the ring of a bell), we build them up after repeated experiences.

Suppose you ordered pizza night after night. When the delivery man presses the doorbell, the digestive juices start flowing even before you can smell the food. Or suppose that you are snuggled up on the couch with your loved one. As you are sitting there staring into the crackling fire, the prospect of feeling close to someone sends your sense of well-being soaring.

There's a children's game that you can use to prove how conditioning works. It goes like this:

Spell out SILK – S, I, L, K.

And again, S, I, L, K. And again, S, I, L, K. And again, S, I, L, K. Now answer this question: What do cows drink?

Most people say 'milk'. Cows, of course, drink water.

What's happening here is that as we become familiar we start to get into a habit. We do the same thing over and over, making it difficult to spot the chance to change. It's like the film *Groundhog Day* – Phil Connors (played by Bill Murray) repeats the same day again and again. Even when he commits suicide it makes no difference, he still wakes up the next morning and has to live through the same day; he realises it's a repeat while everyone else is living it as if for the first time. What about you? What habits and patterns are you in that help to underpin your own expectations and beliefs about the change challenge you have identified?

"We do the same thing over and over, making it difficult to spot the chance to change."

Take a minute to think about the things and people that have influenced you in the formulation of beliefs since the day you were born.

If we are going to understand how to make our beliefs work for us, we must understand where they come from.

You will probably have come up with some or all of the sources in the following list:

- parents
- teachers
- friends
- peers
- leaders
- government
- media
- religion.

Let's look at some of these influences and how they condition us when creating change.

GIGO

Two camels were lazing around, when suddenly the younger camel said to the other, 'Can I ask you a question?'

'Sure,' he said, 'Is there something bothering you?'

'Why do camels have humps?'

The camel paused and reflected. 'Well, we are desert animals. We need the humps to store water. That is how we are able to survive for so long without water.'

'Okay then,' said the first camel, 'so why are our legs long and our feet rounded?'

'Obviously, they are meant for walking in the desert. You know with these legs I can move around the desert better than anyone,' said the older camel with more than a hint of pride.

The quizzical camel nodded his understanding. 'Then why are our eye lashes so long?' he continued. 'Sometimes it bothers my sight.'

'Those long thick eye lashes are your protective cover. They help to protect your eyes from the desert sand and wind,' the wise camel patiently responded.

'I see. So the hump is to store water when we are in the desert, the legs are for walking through the desert and these eye lashes protect my eyes from the desert.' The younger camel listed what he had learned. 'Then what the hell are we doing here in a zoo?'

Unlike the young camel, being able to recognise the effects of our environment is tough. I coach people to be on the lookout for opportunities to regularly get out of their normal environment because at least 70 per cent of what you think about is contained in your immediate environment.

It is possible to do this even when you feel like you don't have a minute to spare and everything seems like a real drag. Why not stop for a second and enjoy some scenery? Pause a while to listen to the sounds of nature? Spend five minutes looking out of your hotel window at the city lights? Admire the view as your aeroplane lands? Take the time to listen to your favourite piece of music while not doing anything else at the same time? Slow down and savour the taste of your lunch without checking phone or email messages? The opportunities to enjoy a moment are out there, but only if you look for them.

Mother Teresa once said that the real horror of life in the slums of Calcutta came not from the daily frustrations and deprivations because people can overcome those. The real nightmare is the effect that the living environment has on beliefs and dreams. If all you see is failure and despair, it is very hard to see the possibilities around you. Albert Einstein said, 'Few people are capable of expressing opinions which differ from the prejudices of their social environment. Most people are even incapable of forming such opinions.'

"If all you see is failure and despair, it is very hard to see the possibilities around you."

Garbage In, Garbage Out (abbreviated to GIGO) is a phrase in the field of computer science that is used to call attention to the fact that computers will unquestioningly process the most nonsensical of inputted data and will consequently produce nonsensical output. The impact of our environment is something that many of us are not consciously aware of, yet it often corresponds with the same computer inputting. If we put garbage into our brains, our performance in creating change will be equally poor.

In 1999 the King of Bhutan, the small, idyllic Buddhist kingdom nestling high in the Himalayas, made a fateful decision: to allow television into his country. Until then TV had been banned, as had all public advertising. But in 1999 the ban on TV was lifted, and licences were given to more than 30 cable operators. The most successful operator provided 46 channels, including Rupert Murdoch's Star TV network. And so the Bhutanese could see the usual mixture of football, violence, sexual betrayal, consumer advertising, wrestling and the like. They lapped it up, but the impact on their society provides a remarkable natural experiment in how technological change can affect attitudes and behaviour.

Quite soon there was a noticeable increase in family break-ups, crime and drug taking. In schools, violence in the playground increased, so much so that one principal's annual report had to include a new section called 'controversies', which reported 'marathon staff meetings' to discuss these new problems. Furthermore, an 'impact study' by some local academics showed that a third of parents now preferred watching TV to talking to their children.

A similar impact was evident from a survey of a thousand 11-year-old children carried out in the late 1990s in England. Two questions were interesting:

1. What is your favourite TV programme?
2. What is your biggest fear?

In the 1960s, when a similar survey was commissioned, the answers to these two respective questions were *Doctor Who* and the Daleks. In the 1990s survey, the answers were *The National Lottery Draw* and being murdered.

Equally disturbing was a study of American television, which has a strong tendency to exaggerate the number of millionaires. In 1982 nearly half of the characters in prime-time social dramas were millionaires. And while two-thirds of real Americans work in blue-collar or service jobs, only 10 per cent of television characters do. This helped to create a culture where many people were conditioned to measure their worth and level of success by the size of their bank account.

Our economy is not immune to the impact of the media either. A ten-year study which looked at the media's portrayal of economic recession concluded that the greater number of times that the word 'recession' appeared in print throughout the ten-year study, the deeper the recession that followed. I suppose it stands to reason that if people read something enough, they start to believe it and behave in recessionary ways in terms of saving, spending and investing.

In addition to the media, it's important to be aware that there are many subtle factors in our environment that can have an influence on the way in which we think, feel and behave. This was demonstrated in a recent study at New York University, where volunteers were asked to rearrange a series of scrambled words to form a coherent sentence. Half of the participants were shown mixed-up sentences that contained words relating to the elderly, such as 'man's was skin the wrinkled'.

The other half of the participants were shown the same mixed sentences, but the one word relating to the elderly was replaced with a word not normally associated with old age, such as 'man's was skin the smooth'.

Once a participant had worked their way through the sentences and been thanked for taking part in the test, they were given directions to the nearest set of elevators.

Although the participants didn't realise it, they were then timed to see how long it took to reach the elevators. Those who had spent time unscrambling the sentences relating to old age took significantly longer than those who had spent time with the non-elderly sentences. Just spending a few minutes thinking about words such as 'wrinkled' and 'grey' had completely changed the way people behaved.

Change action

So how does your environment impact on your belief in your own ability to create change?

Try answering this yourself by keeping tabs on the types of information (TV programmes, newspapers) you absorb during the next week and ask yourself how the programmes you watch and the stories you read impact on you.

There was a disturbing example of this kind of impact in 1998, when some headline-grabbing stories in the UK suggested a possible link between MMR immunity jabs for babies and the onset of autism. The MMR jab is vital for preventing epidemics of measles, mumps and rubella, measles being the most worrying. On the basis of these newspaper reports a huge number of new parents refused to allow their babies to receive the jab, not wishing to take the risk.

▶

In fact, the scare story came from a single paediatrician who observed 12 autistic children with bowel disease and suggested that the autism *may* be connected to the measles virus in the MMR vaccine. In fact, when the possible link to autism was later tested across the world with millions of children, it was seen to be entirely unfounded. There was no link, no support for the single doctor's hypothesis and it was even pointed out that the rise in autism cases had happened before the MMR vaccine was introduced.

We are now in a situation where children are being put at risk because of the resulting drop in vaccination levels to well below what is needed to protect the population at large. In an open letter to newspapers following a massive increase in childhood deaths from measles, the experts said, 'Unless this is rectified urgently and children are immunised, we will see more unnecessary deaths.' How many headlines do you think these facts received?

Relationships

There is a story about the famous scientist Albert Einstein, which all parents would do well to remember. Young Albert, apparently, didn't say a single word as a baby or toddler. In fact, he didn't say anything during his first four years. Naturally his parents started to get very worried and had him referred to all kinds of specialists, but to no avail. Then, one day, out of the blue, little Albert came out with his first utterance, the fully formed sentence, 'This soup is too hot!'

After they had got over their general rejoicing and relief, Herr and Frau Einstein turned to their son and said, 'But why have you not spoken, up to now?' The boy shrugged and said, '*Bis jetzt, alles in Ordung.*' (Which, roughly translated, means, 'Well, up to now everything's been okay.')

As an adult, he paid tribute to the influence of his parents and their constant encouragement when he said, 'The good effects of their early teachings and belief I can never lose. They never misunderstood or misjudged me.'

The nature of our relationships with the significant people in our life is hugely important in helping us to become a change catalyst. Let me explain.

Psychologists suggest that during the conversations we have with others, we make signals or 'bids'. If that word makes you think of a poker game or an auction room, then you're on the right track. A bid is something that invites a response. Often, we don't notice how we are responding – until it is too late and the damage has been done.

"A bid is something that invites a response."

The good news is that these micro signals (or 'bids') are very easy to spot and pretty easy to change if we know where to look and are willing to make the effort.

This was demonstrated in a study carried out in the early 1980s by psychologist John Gottman, who researched why some married couples stay together while others break up. Professor Gottman watched a series of couples closely as they went about their daily interactions and found that the answer he was looking for lay in the tiny details of those apparently inconsequential everyday exchanges. Banal as they seemed on the surface, at another level they were highly nuanced emotional exchanges.

The impact of Gottman's work was enormous. Based on his insights a whole new approach to marriage counselling was developed. So how does this work and how is it related to creating change?

Picture the scene. Your partner is sitting in front of their computer, working away. You enter the room and ask whether they fancy a coffee. Your partner now has the chance to respond in one of three ways:

1. **They could acknowledge your offer and reply to it in a positive way.** 'That's really kind. I'll have it black with lots of sugar.' Or, 'Thanks, but I'm okay right now.' In psychologist speak, this is called a 'turning towards' response or a 'response' bid.

2. **They could acknowledge it in a negative way.** 'Your coffee is disgusting, I'll do it myself.' Or, 'You want to make me a coffee? What do you want in return?' Unsurprisingly, this is called an 'against' bid.

3. **They could just stay silent, or reply by changing the subject.** 'There is a new film out this week.' This is called an 'away from' bid. By replying they acknowledge that you have spoken, but they don't engage with what you've said. In effect they ignore your bid.

Whatever response they choose will determine what you do next. But only the first one is likely to encourage you to make another bid. Faced with an 'against' or 'away from' bid, we are more likely to make an unconscious mental note not to bother asking next time.

The research shows that when we use plenty of the 'turning towards' responses, the effects are enormous. Couples where the exchanges are predominantly 'towards' stay together. In fact, there is even a magic ratio. If we manage a ratio of 5:1 positive ('towards') responses to negative ('away from' or 'against') responses, we are likely to have a healthy, long-lasting partnership.

"When we use plenty of the 'turning towards' responses, the effects are enormous."

This ratio is also important in the workplace. In a recent survey, 99 out of 100 people reported that they wanted to be around positive people, and nine out of ten reported being more productive when they are around positive people. This is supported by another recent study which found that workplaces with positive-to-negative ratios greater than 3:1 are significantly more productive than teams that don't reach this ratio.

Change action

We have already learned that the people we surround ourselves with play a significant part in determining how much self-belief we have, and we also know that having self-belief is critical when attempting to bring about change. Learning the language of bids helps us analyse whether we are surrounding ourselves with the right type of people to assist us on our change mission.

Think of someone specific who is important to helping you to create change and count how many times you make a response/away from/against bid in one day.

Are you at the magic ratio of 5:1 for response bids versus away from/against bids? If so, there is little work to be done here and you can be assured that this person is likely to assist you in your mission to bring about change. If you haven't hit this ratio, you can attempt to improve the relationship by increasing the number of response bids that you make and they may well follow your example.

The knowledge bank

Another way to foster beliefs is through seeking knowledge. A direct experience is one form of knowledge. Another is gained through reading, seeing movies and viewing the world as it is portrayed by others. Knowledge is one of the great ways to break the shackles of a limiting environment. No matter how grim your world is, if you can read about the accomplishments of others, you can create the beliefs that will allow you to succeed.

For example, have you ever dreamed of being a writer? My hero and guiding light in this respect is a Frenchman, Jean-Dominique Bauby. He wrote an extraordinarily observant book, *The Diving Bell and the Butterfly*. Bauby, who was a *bon viveur* and editor-in-chief of French magazine *Elle*, was suddenly plunged at the age of 43 into a locked-in syndrome where the only organ he could move was his left eye. His mind was alive but nothing else. He dictated his brilliant book by blinking to indicate each letter to spell out a word. He died of a heart attack on 19 March 1997, two days after his book was published. I keep a copy of this book at my writing table and if I am ever struggling to write, this hero of mine puts things into perspective.

What are your favourite books and films? How do they inspire you?

Self-consistency theory

Another way to establish beliefs to help you create change is through identifying your best change-making behaviours. Just as past experiences change your beliefs about what is possible, so can your imagined experiences of what you want things to be in the future. This is where we started this book when identifying your best behaviours.

You

Finally, we come to the most important of all factors: you.

We have looked at a number of factors that create and mobilise beliefs. Most of us form our beliefs haphazardly. We soak things up – good and bad – from the world around us. But one of the key ideas of this book is that you're not just a leaf in the wind. You can control your conditioning and in turn control your beliefs, your attitudes, your feelings and your behaviour to become a change catalyst.

The single most important conditioning factor in our lives therefore is ourselves. You see, we actually have absolute and total control over how we process every single external thing that we experience.

"The single most important conditioning factor in our lives is ourselves."

Change action

There are two things that you can do about your conditioning. In Disney's *The Lion King*, Rafiki, the wise old baboon, tries to persuade Simba to return home and save his pride. Simba, who believes that he is responsible for the death of his father, refuses because he thinks people won't understand. Rafiki looks at him and tells him that his father's death is in the past and he must move on. Simba says that he can't.

Rafiki then takes the stick that he carries around with him and hits Simba on the head. Simba roars in pain and asks why he did it. Rafiki looks at him, shrugs and says, 'It doesn't matter; it's in the past!' Then he takes another swipe but this time Simba is waiting and ducks to avoid the blow. Rafiki laughs and says, 'The way I see it, you can either run from the past or you can learn from it.'

The first thing is to change how you think about your past conditioning. The point is, whatever you have said or done in the past is history. You cannot change it so don't beat yourself up over it. Learn from it so you don't make the same mistake again and then move on to make the changes that are important to you.

The second point is that **you can change how you think about every single piece of conditioning with which you are confronted from now on. If someone tells you that the change you desire is impossible, it's up to you whether you accept it or not.**

Eleanor Roosevelt once said, 'No one can insult you without your consent.' It is the same with conditioning. No one can condition you without your consent. You just have to be aware of it.

Step **10**

'New ideas often appear first as jokes, then as blasphemies
and treason and finally as established truths.'

George Bernard Shaw

Take action: over to you...

Knowledge is like having money in the bank. It is valuable but it is not, by itself, useful. Only when the money is converted into something does it become useful. The good news is that, unlike money, knowledge actually appreciates when you spend it, creating new insights and more knowledge. It is a bit like getting richer by going shopping.

"Knowledge actually appreciates when you spend it, creating new insights and more knowledge."

Whatever you have taken from this book is the same. Without action, it is fairly pointless. For example, it is all very well knowing how to recognise the four types of people in your life. It takes energy and courage to do something positive with this information.

Research by Robert Brinkerhoff suggests that after attending a typical training course, only 15 per cent of people are still adopting the lessons a few months later. With a book it's even less. Why?

One answer lies in the work of the nineteenth-century German philosopher Arthur Schopenhauer, who suggested that taking action to make change happen has three clear stages:

1. It is ridiculed
2. It is violently opposed
3. It is accepted as self-evident.

A great example of how these three stages work can be found in the inspiring example of Cliff Young.

Every year, Australia hosts 550-mile endurance racing from Sydney to Melbourne, which is considered among the world's most gruelling ultra-marathons. The race takes five days to complete and is normally only attempted by world-class athletes who train specially for the event. These athletes are typically less than 30 years old and backed by large sportswear companies.

In 1983 Cliff Young showed up at the start of this race. Cliff was 61 years old and wore work overalls and a pair of Wellington boots. To everyone's surprised amusement, he wasn't a spectator. He picked up his race number and joined the other runners.

The press and other athletes became curious and questioned Cliff. They laughingly told him, 'You're crazy, there's no way you can finish this race.' To which he replied, 'Yes, I can. See, I grew up on a farm where we couldn't afford horses or tractors, and the whole time I was growing up, whenever the storms would roll in, I'd have to go out and round up the sheep. We had 2000 sheep on 2000 acres. Sometimes I would have to run those sheep for two or three days. It took a long time, but I'd always catch them. I believe I can run this race.'

When the race started, the professionals quickly left Cliff behind. The crowds and television audience were entertained because Cliff didn't even run properly; he appeared to shuffle. Many even feared for the old farmer's well-being.

All of the professional athletes knew that it took about five days to finish the race. In order to compete, the athletes had to run about 18 hours a day and sleep the remaining six hours. The thing is, Cliff Young didn't know that!

When the morning of the second day came, everyone was in for another surprise. Not only was Cliff still in the race, he had continued jogging all night. Eventually Cliff was asked about his tactics for the rest of the race. To everyone's disbelief, he claimed he would run straight through to the finish without sleeping. And he kept running. Each night he came a little closer to the leading pack and he moved from Schopenhauer's stage one to stage two of change, as the officials' reaction was to consult the rule book to see if he had broken the rules. They discovered that it was only convention which dictated that runners must sleep for six hours.

By the final night, he had surpassed all of the young, world-class athletes. He was the first competitor to cross the finish line and he set a new course record. When he was awarded the winning prize of $10,000, he said he didn't know there was a prize and insisted that he did not enter for the money. He ended up giving all of his winnings to several other runners, an act that endeared him to all of Australia.

Today, the 'Cliff Young shuffle' has been adopted by most ultra-marathon runners because it is considered more energy efficient. At least three champions of the Sydney to Melbourne race have used the shuffle to win and it is now accepted that competitors do not sleep. Winning the race requires runners to run all night as well as all day, just like Cliff Young. He changed the world of ultra-marathon running for ever.

Enduring these three stages of change takes courage, but why do so few people successfully make change happen?

A clue is found by looking at the second most common phobia in the UK (behind our fear of spiders): *sociophobia*. This is the official name given to the fear of embarrassment or ridicule by others. Unfortunately, when creating change, ridicule often comes first. It is also often the first stage of change where most people fail and give up.

"Unfortunately, when creating change, ridicule often comes first."

Go back to the start of the book and remind yourself of your very best behaviours, the words that define how you want to be perceived and then follow the structure of understanding and controlling your emotions, recognise the facts of the situation and your own and others' response to them before looking at your beliefs and determining whether they help or hinder you. Finally, analyse your environment to ensure that it is structured to facilitate the change you want to see. Then, act with courage to implement the actions.

In 1978 Mother Teresa accepted the Nobel Peace Prize for the courage and inspiration she demonstrated in changing the lives of those living within the slums of Calcutta. She quoted Dr Kent Keith's Paradoxical Commandments which are an appropriate place to leave you to go and take on your own change challenge:

People are illogical, unreasonable, and self-centered.
Love them anyway.

If you do good, people will accuse you of selfish ulterior motives.
Do good anyway.

If you are successful, you will win false friends and true enemies.
Succeed anyway.

The good you do today will be forgotten tomorrow.
Do good anyway.

Honesty and frankness make you vulnerable.
Be honest and frank anyway.

The biggest men and women with the biggest ideas can be shot down by the smallest men and women with the smallest minds.
Think big anyway.

People favour underdogs but follow only top dogs.
Fight for a few underdogs anyway.

What you spend years building may be destroyed overnight.
Build anyway.

People really need help but may attack you if you do help them.
Help people anyway.

Give the world the best you have and you'll get kicked in the teeth.
Give the world the best you have anyway.

Good luck.

Personal postscript

Thank you for buying this book. If it somehow exceeded your expectations or left you thinking, 'Wow, things would be better if more people read it,' this section is just for you.

Putting into practice the advice I have been dispensing within these pages, I want to see if you can help inspire change with me.

A number of years ago, I left the safe confines of the corporate world, where I was earning a living as a human resources director, because I had a dream of being independent and of taking my ideas and beliefs to a wider audience. My purpose was (and still is) to help inspire people and teams to go further than they believe possible. I thought I could do this by writing books, speaking to audiences and working within teams as a coach and adviser.

I could fill another book about the conflicting advice I received as I contemplated making the break away from the guaranteed monthly payments, pension and other benefits of working within big business, but I had this nagging thought that I didn't want to 'die with the music still in me', a phrase coined by the famous rugby league coach Wayne Bennett. With my heart in my mouth, I decided to risk it and handed in my notice.

I won't detail the journey, suffice to say I have been fortunate enough to enjoy many highlights. Above all, it has been having the opportunity to meet people and make many wonderful friends while following my dream.

Still, I am a young, independent author. I don't have a huge marketing machine behind me, or a gang of billionaire friends, or even a magic genie offering me three wishes. But that is okay. If you are willing to offer a few minutes of your time, you can seriously help this book move forward on its journey to reach all of the people it should.

Please consider doing any of the following:

1. Write a review on amazon.co.uk.
2. Post about this book on your blog, Facebook, LinkedIn or Twitter.
3. Recommend this book to your co-workers, your friends and your friends' friends, or your friends who blog, or even your friends of friends who blog about their friends' blogs. You get the idea. The possibilities are endless.
4. If you know people who write for newspapers or magazines, drop them a line.
5. Check out www.liquidthinker.com and register for my newsletter to discover all the great things I write about. If you like what you find, run through this list again with that in mind.

Although it might feel negligible, doing any of the above will make a huge difference. As the author, my opinion of this book carries surprisingly little weight. But you, dear reader, have all the power in the world.

Not only can you help this book find its way, but for me you'd also make the many risks of writing my next book easier to overcome, increasing the odds that I'll do an even better job next time around.

As always, thanks for your help and support.

Damian Hughes

damian@liquidthinker.com

Bringing Damian Hughes to your organisation

Damian Hughes speaks at team events and conferences and conducts seminars and masterclasses. He tailors his message to your requirements and is commonly asked to speak on the psychology of leadership, high performing teams, winning cultures and change.

For more details about booking Damian, either:

Email: damian@liquidthinker.com

Or visit: www.liquidthinker.com

If you prefer, you can telephone the offices of LiquidThinker Ltd. on +44 (0)7939122120

We look forward to hearing from you.

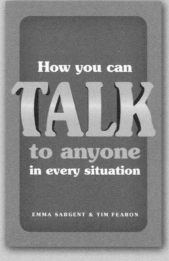
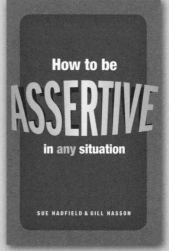